The Isle of Vaila

Volume 1 - A Miscellany

The Isle of Vaila

Volume 1

A Miscellany

Richard Rowland

Vaila Fine Art
Lerwick
2008

The Isle of Vaila, Volume 1, A Miscellany

First Edition 2008.

Published by Vaila Fine Art, 61 Commercial Street, Lerwick, Shetland ZE1 0AB.
www.vailafineart.co.uk

All characters and events in this book are based on real people and actual events. No attempt has been made to protect the identities of the guilty; the innocent need no protection anyway.

A CIP catalogue record for this book is available from the British Library.

ISBN 978-0-9560748-0-5

Cover photographs: Front – Isle of Vaila from the south-east;
Inside front – Isle of Vaila from the north-west (John Coutts);
Inside back – Quiet evening at Vaila Hall, Richard, Dorota and Effie;
Back – Navigational map (Dave Donaldson).

Printed by
Shetland Litho,
Gremista, Lerwick,
Shetland, ZE1 0PX.

Vaila from Burrastow.
Photograph: Didier Piquer

Antony Bream
"Portrait of the author", 2007,
charcoal, 14 x 18 inches.

This book is dedicated to my wife Dorota Rychlik who has found her spiritual home on the Isle of Vaila and in so doing follows the tradition of the strong woman of the Northern Isles.

Dorota going for a spin with Olga in Richard Price's 1934 Rolls- Royce 20/25 H.P. Barker Sedancalette de Ville.
Photograph: Richard Rowland

The Isle of Vaila

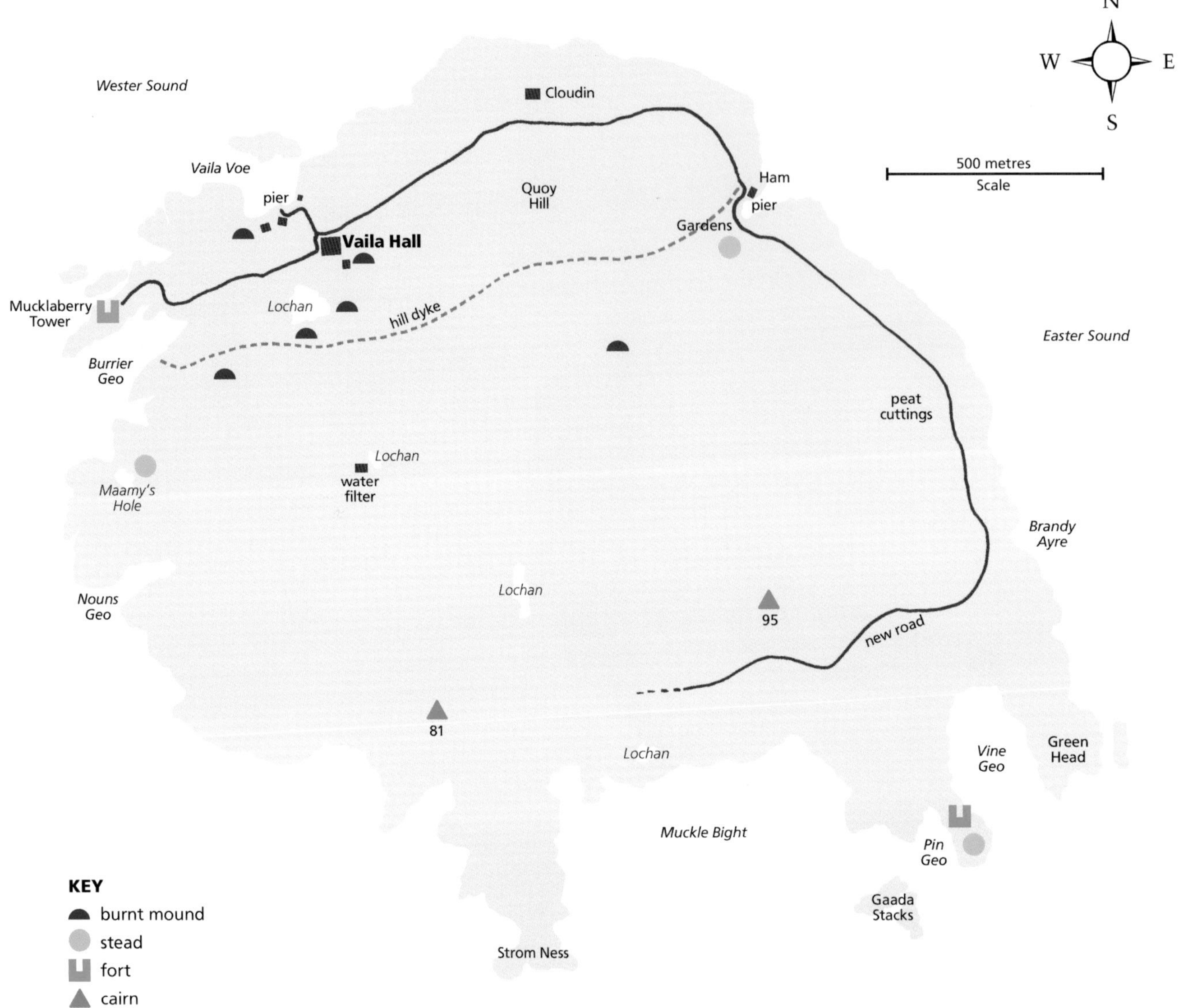

Chapter 1

The Isle of Vaila

Vaila rather fell into our lap. We were not looking for an island; just an old pile to restore. And our decision to buy was hardly rational; but then those are the best decisions.

The description in Historic Scotland's list of Buildings at Risk was intriguing. So we booked flights for our first visit to Shetland in October 1992. Henry Anderton, the laird who with his wife Bo owned and ran Burrastow House Hotel across the sound from Vaila was away, so cunningly arranged for us to be booked into the Westings Hotel at Weisdale and Whiteness; it has no claims on the Cipriani, but its views over the west side of Shetland are staggering. Freddy Georgeson and his mother-in-law Laura, who was born on the island, took us over from Burrastow in Henry's aluminium voe boat on quite a blustery day to show us around.

We were entranced; here was a Victorian time warp, on which 20th century civilisation and conveniences had barely intruded. The Great Hall was furnished as it was in 1900, the ancient generator spluttered into life at the flick of a switch, the roof was not leaking, but the solid fuel (peat) central heating system installed for a mere £176 in 1900 had long retired, and the house which had not seen regular habitation for about 12 years was as cold as a grave.

Of course the Condition Report by our architects, Nick and Limma Groves-Raines brought us back to reality, but the possibilities were legion. The house was basically sound, it was Grade B listed, so permission for repairs and improvements was possible, and most importantly it was habitable; running a restoration project at long range would have been very difficult. And being on its own island, only 10 minutes from the mainland was the gilding on the lily.

One of our first visitors was my cousin Nick Cowdery, never one to avoid stating the obvious, who remarked "You'll have your work cut out here." This is not intended to be a "We bought an island" book so you will be spared the details of his prediction, but a general summary of our work programme appears later.

Another prediction by locals was that we would not survive long on the island; but then they had not met anyone like Dorota before.

Rather this book's genesis comes from folders we prepared for guests of Frequently Asked Questions, since the repetition of information about the island was becoming tedious. So the real aim is to provide answers to these and assemble together many of the disparate articles, stories, writings, photographs and paintings of and about Vaila, and a sketch of its history and inhabitants and flora and fauna. Remarkably, it is likely that there has been continuous habitation on Vaila for some 4,500 years, so I have used a rather broad brush.

I will however underline two themes, in case you don't spot them.

Firstly that the early English were possibly settling in Shetland since before the Vikings, and English is of course now the main language. This provides some explanation why Shetlanders seem to accept English "soothmoothers" like me with good grace. Perhaps there is some common ancestry, although their natural good humour, wry understanding, soft spoken approach and incredible industry are traits which could be exported south with advantage.

The other theme relates to the role of the strong woman in the Northern Isles. In 1299 Ragnvald Simunsdottar who lived on Papa Stour, a nearby island, was taking on the Norwegian King's factor with great confidence over a rent dispute, declaiming him as a "Judas."

And the Ballad of Hildina, in oral tradition from about 1200 and in Orkney and Shetland Norn, describes how the King of Norway's daughter poisoned her entire (second) wedding party in the Northern Isles including her new husband largely because he had thrown her first husband's severed head to her like a rugger ball.

My wife, Dorota is definitely in this tradition. But without her enormous energy, insatiable appetite for projects and infectious sense of humour, all on Vaila would be but dust.

First time visitors to Vaila often want to plan an entertainment programme, involving trips and tours to take in the sights around Shetland. But after a day or two on the island these plans usually come to naught; visitors rarely leave the island until they have to. I think the main reason for this, apart from Dorota's hospitality, is that Vaila is a microcosm of all that is best about Shetland; space, peace, natural beauty and wonderful light. And writing this on an exquisite evening at my desk in the bell-tower, with its semi-circular leaded windows catching the sunset out to Vaila Voe, Wester Sound and Mucklaberry Tower, it is very hard to trump the place.

But I hope that you, dear reader, will keep this a closely guarded secret.

Chapter 2

Auld Rocks

Vaila is part of the Caledonian mountain range, forced into existence by the collision of two tectonic plates about 420 million years ago. Eroding over many millions of years the resulting rocks and stones were compressed together to form layers of Old Red Sandstone. In turn these layers fault to create innumerable ledges, as on the cliffs by Mucklaberry Tower.

Mucklaberry Tower guarding the entrance to Wester Sound.

Cliffs at Mucklaberry Tower; the fault lines in the Old Red Sandstone form ideal ledges for nesting birds.

Cliffs on the south of Vaila; Old Red Sandstone to the left and Red Granite to the right.

Gaada Stacks on the south side of Vaila.

At the same time volcanic activity would have created molten rocks, such as the Red Granite which appears on the southern extremity of Vaila, adjacent to the Gaada stacks.

Geological Sketch Map of Shetland

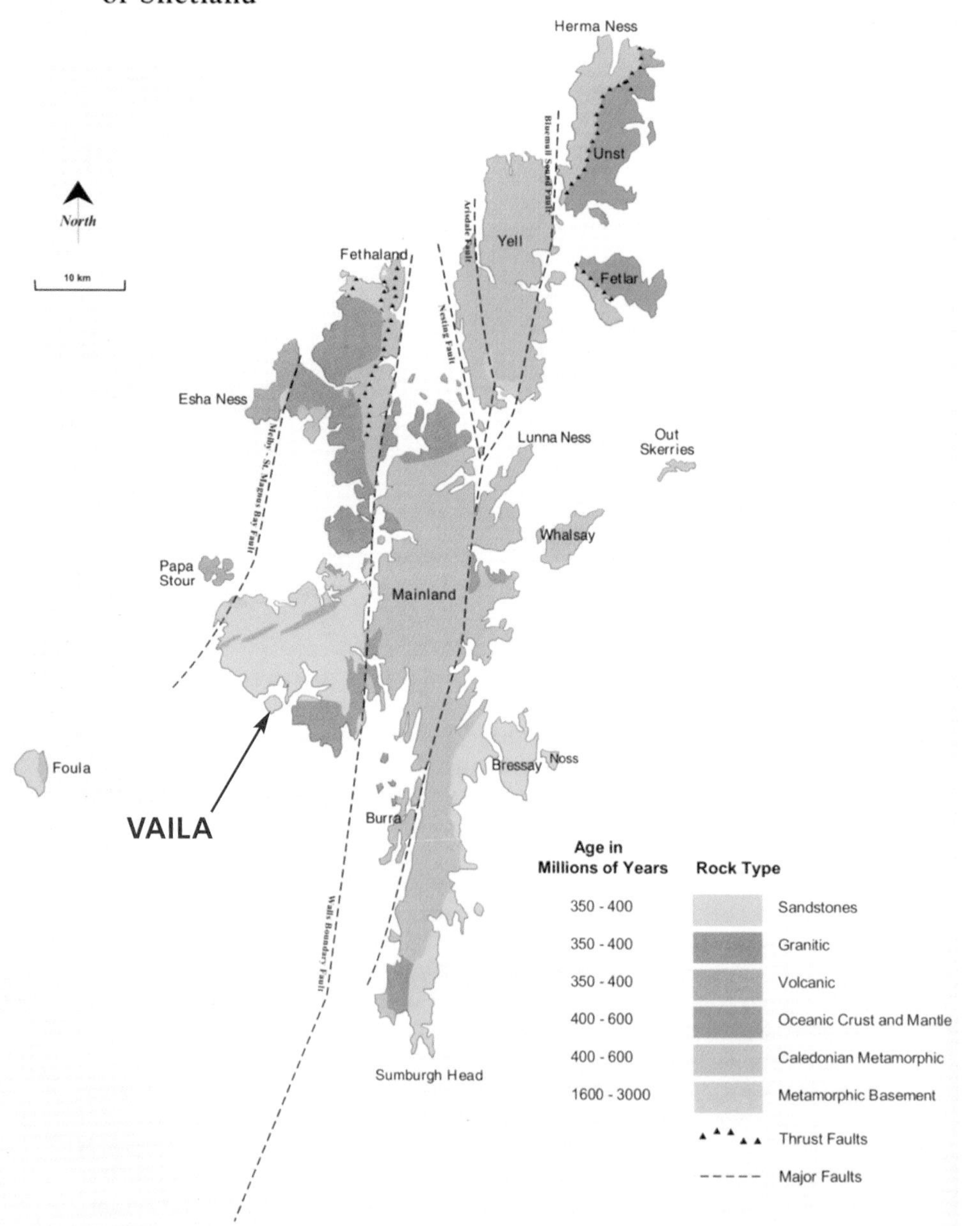

Geological map of Shetland; Vaila is primarily Old Red Sandstone, except for Red Granite in the South-east corner.

This represents the western end of a large area of Red Granite on the Culswick and Skeld peninsular to the east of Vaila.

The faults in the cliffs on the west and south of Vaila have allowed the sea to erode them, and create large caves at sea level. In time their roofs have weakened and collapsed, as at Maamy's Hole, south of Mucklaberry Tower.

Maamy's hole; our spectacular blow-hole on the west side of Vaila.

The last ice age in Shetland finished about 10,000 years ago. Much of the relatively smooth contours of Vaila were created by glaciation, for example, the valley between the two highest points on Vaila, 91m and 82m high respectively, as well as the small lochans.

Also the ice would have depressed the land, so that on melting, the sea level rose, creating the voes around Vaila, to leave it completely surrounded by water. As a result the north coast of Vaila was sheltered from erosion, whilst on the rocky south west coast the sea formed inlets or geos such as Burriers Geo and Nouns Geo, as well as caves in Muckle Bight on the south and from Green Head to Brandy Ayre on the south east. The sea has a depth of about 30m immediately offshore Vaila, increasing to about 80m about 800m offshore

For over 7,000 years peat has been accumulating on parts of Vaila, but not on the more fertile parks along the north coast and at the top of the cliffs from Stromness to Green Head on the south coast. Most of the more recent peat cuttings are on the north-east slopes of the east ward hill.

There are four lochans on Vaila, the deepest between mid ward and east ward. We stocked this one with 500 trout smoults. But approaching it once with my rod for a quiet days fishing, I saw a large otter scurry into the lochan: he was using it as a fridge and must have thought it was Christmas when the smoults arrived. I never caught any.

The lochan further north is now a holding tank for our filtration system for hill water used in the house. The water passes through carbon filters, but never loses its brown tinge from the peat it flows through. Our guests soon get used to bathing in water the colour of light mud. Drinking water comes from a well outside the back door of the Hall, quite delicious with a high mineral content.

The island comprises some 800 acres and is shaped rather like a jelly fish with a diameter of about 2km. The northern quarter is bisected by the hill dyke, separating the hill, moorland and peat banks to the south from the "improved" pasture to the north.

We were the first farm in Shetland to gain organic status in 1994. Part of the conditions to support our benefiting from being in an Environmentally Sensitive Area is that mowing in some of the improved parks must be delayed until August, after the corncrakes have nested. Nobody seems bothered by the fact that corncrakes have not been seen on Vaila for many years. They are not an endangered species; there are millions of them in the Gulag. Anyway they are welcome to nest on the island.

But I am jumping ahead of myself; we must go back in time to our forbears on the island.

Chapter 3

Early Settlement

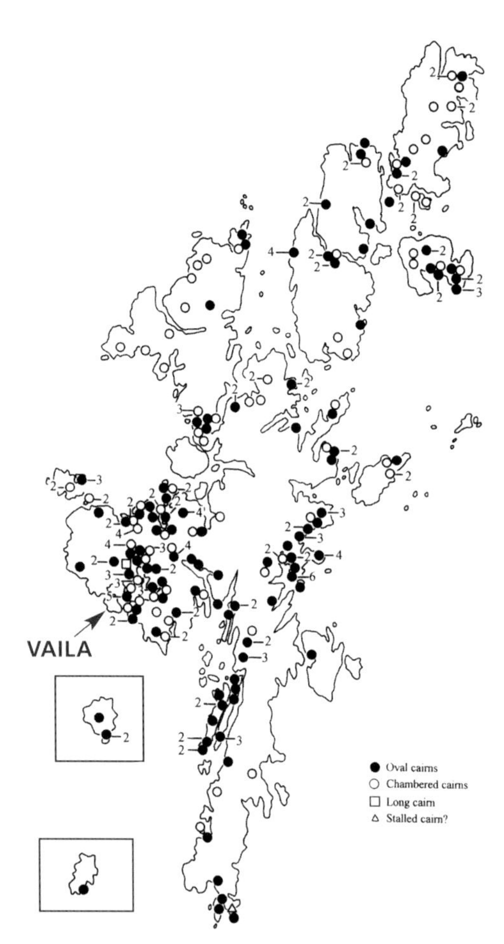

Prehistoric houses and cairns on Shetland.

In the Mesolithic period between 10,000 and 7,000 B.C. light woodland would have become established on Shetland, mainly hazel, willow, rowan and juniper. There may have been nomadic settlement along the coast. However as the sea level has risen about 5m since then, no evidence of Mesolithic settlement has been found.

From about 4,000 B.C. when the temperature was about 3˚C higher than today, farming was established on the west-side of Shetland. The Scord of Brouster, near Bridge of Walls, has been excavated revealing houses, fields and clearance cairns, generally used for arable crops such as beere (barley) as well as sheep and cattle. The land was ploughed with an Ard, a simple plough with a stone tipped end, pulled by cows. Stone dykes divided the fields or rigs and also the hill land. Possibly Shetland had some 10,000 inhabitants during the next 2000 years or so.

The map of prehistoric houses and cairns shows large clusters on the west-side, but none on Vaila. However it is likely that Vaila would have had its share of settlements. A survey by the Shetland Field Studies Group organised by Jill Slee Blackadder identified over 20 potential sites. There are some seven burnt mounds and possibly three "steads"; the one adjacent to Maamy's Hole has been surveyed and mapped by Val Turner.

The two largest burnt mounds are by the west pier and behind the Hall, both well watered by burns from the hill and the well beside the Hall. So it is possible that there were settlements in the areas now covered by the Hall and its outbuildings and the sheds near the west pier.

The usage of burnt mounds, which are conical mounds of shale from stones shattered by heating and cooling is not proven. One such use would be by putting heated stones in water in stone troughs for cooking. Experiments have shown that Jamie Oliver would not rate this as efficient. Another usage would be to create a basic sauna, in the nature of a North American sweat lodge; another is tanning. Dorota's theory is that they were either early beauty parlours, or could have been used by mothers wishing to give their children a

The largest burnt mound on Vaila, near the west pier.

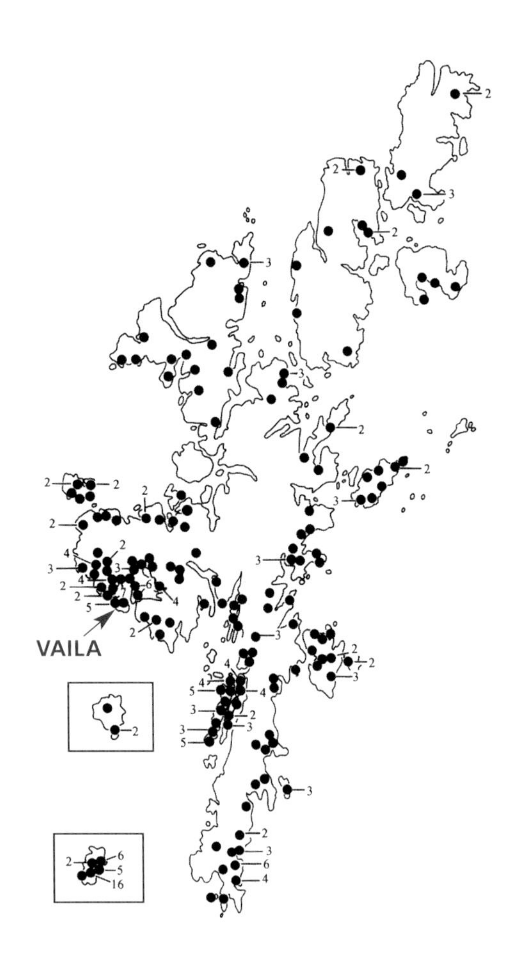

Burnt mounds in Shetland.

warm water birth. Whatever it is, our prehistoric ancestors must have been busy cooking, tanning or sweating away on Vaila.

By about 3,000 B.C. the temperature had fallen by about 2˚C and moorland and blanket peat was spreading over Shetland, caused by the general clearing of woodland, over-farming resulting in the loss of good pasture, and in turn less manure and generally greater acidity. The settlers were forced into smaller settlements, creating competition for land. This may have encouraged the building of "forts" for protection, like that at Burgi Geo on a peninsular in Yell ; a sketch of this in 1853 shows similarities with the remains on the promontory between Vine Geo and Pin Geo on the south east of Vaila. By about 500 B.C. to 500 A.D. during the Iron Age, the climate may have improved. Brochs were built at some time in this period; there are about 120 in Shetland, all on the coast. These dry stone built circular convex pepper pots similar to nuclear cooling towers have two skins of stone, with galleries for storage. There were no windows and the entrance was through a low doorway at ground level. Across Easter Sound from Vaila lies Culswick broch with its distinctive triangular shaped lintel. It was described by George Low in 1774 as then 5m high, after many stones had been removed for house building. By comparison the most complete broch remaining in Shetland at Mousa is now 13m high. There was also a much smaller broch at the point of Burrastow, but none on Vaila. We

Burgi Geos (sketch 1853). (RCAHMS)

Remains on the promontory between Vine Geo and Pin Geo on the south of Vaila.

partially remedied this by building a 20th century broch in the style of Mousa broch, about 4m high, at our shorebase in Lera Voe. It was opened by Val Turner in 1997, and is now used for oil storage. Our press release for this appears in Chapter 7.

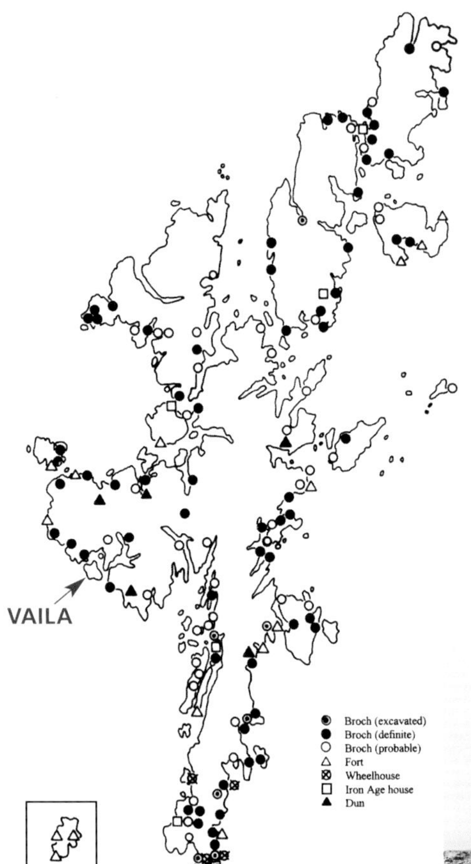

Brochs on Shetland.

Culswick broch, south east of Vaila.

Our broch, built in 1997 at Vaila Shorebase, Lera Voe, Burrastow.

In the Pictish period (500-800 A.D.) the weather deteriorated again, but Christianity was brought to Shetland to cheer things up, as evidenced by stones found at Bressay, Papil and St Ninian's Isle. There were a number of monastic sites on promontories; adjacent to Culswick broch are stacks in Buri Geo which were inhabited by monks or hermits. It is possible that the promontory on Vaila between Vine Geo and Pin Geo could have served the same purpose. Certainly normal habitation would have been difficult there. It is now on the approach to the green on the spectacular 700 yards, par 6, 16th hole on the back nine of our golf course.

Monastic site on stacks off Buri Geo.

Any well informed reader of 1066 and All That will know of the invasion of Britain in about 450 A.D. by Hengist and his shadowy brother Horsa, starting the settlement of Britain by the early English, namely Jutes, Angles and Saxons. What is little known is that this duo also possibly subdued Orkney with 40 ships in 443 A.D. as described in the History of Britain by the Welsh monk Nennius, 9th century A.D. (See quotation in Chapter 7).

There may have been subsequent settlement of the Northern Isles by the early English. Genetic surveys show a footprint of one third Viking and two thirds others, which could include these early English settlers, as well as existing settlers with a similar genetic make up.

The Vikings started raiding in about 790 A.D. and subsequently settled throughout Shetland. King Harald 1 of Norway annexed Orkney and Shetland in 875 A.D. and created the Jarls of Orkney and Lords of Shetland to govern the islands.

The weather was better between 1000-1300 A.D. and in this period farming was established under Norse practices, involving Scattald, or common grazings, and land ownership under Udal law. Orkney and Shetland were governed by Norse earls, and after 1195 Shetland was administered by the King of Norway. There is little written evidence from this period. One piece is a document from 1299 held by the Arnamagnaean Institute in the University of Copenhagen concerning a claim by Ragnhild Simunsdatter about rentals payable on the Norwegian King's farm at Bragaster on Papa Stour, which was administered and collected by Thorvald Thoresson. The claim was determined in favour of Thorvald at the Lawting in Tingwall. It evidences a complex system of administration and rentals, payable in corn.

It is highly likely that Vaila would at that time have been settled by Norse folk, and administered by Norse landowners, or the Norwegian crown. It is also quite possible that a Norwegian Stofa, or communal building, similar to that excavated at Biggins, Papa Stour, was built on Vaila, probably on the site of the Hall.

Although Norse power lessened after the 13th century, it had effectively removed Celtic influences, including language, forced Christianity underground, and seen the development of Orkney and Shetland Norn as the language of the Northern Isles.

By about 1400 there were a number of languages in use in Shetland; Old Norse, being the spoken and written language of the Norwegian ruling class; the Papa Stour document of 1299 is the first surviving example of this relating to Shetland. Also Scots Gaelic, with its Pictish ancestry, which was dying out. And Orkney and Shetland Norn, spoken, not written, as developed from pre-Viking settlers. Interestingly this Orkney and Shetland Norn was the only Germanic based language which did not undergo the "i-mutation" of all other Germanic based languages (evidenced by plural forms such as foot to feet and goose to geese) in the period 1450-1500 A.D. possibly showing its isolation in this period and more importantly the common use of Germanic based languages there before then. Of course linguistic archaeology is difficult to prove or disprove since no recordings of contemporary speech survive.

So perhaps the real legacy of these early English settlers stemming from Hengist and Horsa was language. By the 17th century, the influence of the Norwegians had gone and was replaced by the Scots. Significantly these were mainly lowland Scots whose main language was English. So this combined with the similar language of the early English settlers, and helped by being the language of the ruling class, as well as being written, with the Bible to promote it, made it the surviving language of Shetland.

However the name Vaila, now popular as a Shetland girls' name, comes from Val-øy. Øy is Old Norse for island and Valr for falcon. It also appears in old documents as Valay and Walo. Other meanings for Valr are horse, battlefield and as an adjective, round.

Chapter 4

An abstract of title to Vaila

Not many home owners can deduce their title to the 15th century; but we can. By about 1450 a number of Norwegian landowners held major estates in Shetland, based on the isles of Papa Stour, Vaila and Noss. One such "Lord of Norway" was Sigurd Johnson of Giske. He died in 1453, and his son Hans in 1466, without issue. His estates in Norway and Shetland were divided between the three heirs of Sigurd's two sisters. On 11th September 1490 this disposition was recorded in a document executed under seal in Bergen; this confirmed the title of one of the heirs, Alv Knutsson's to Vaila amongst other lands. (FN1)

Prior to this, on 28th May 1469 King Christian of Denmark had granted a mortgage to King James of Scotland as security for the dowry for his daughter, of his royal rights in Shetland, "until the sum of 8000 Florins has been faithfully paid in the Church of St Magnus in Orkney whensoever in the future ..." (FN2)

King Christian also wrote at the same time to the inhabitants of Orkney and Shetland asking them to be "obedient and dutiful to (the King of Scotland) until such time as ... the money for which the said lands and islands were mortgaged" have been repaid. (FN3) Unfortunately the mortgage did not have a term, so failing repayment, an Act of Annexation to the Scots crown of the Earldom of Orkney and the Lordship of Shetland was passed in Edinburgh on 20th February 1471/2. (FN4)

Alv Knutsson's great grand-daughter, Gorvel Fadersdotter, another example of a strong woman who at one stage held the largest estates in Norway succeeded to the Vaila estate and in 1563 Vincent Hawick was collecting rent for her (FN5). In 1572 she leased Vaila to Robert Cheyne (FN6), confirmed by letters under privy seal at Holyroodhouse dated 3rd March 1575/6. This document refers to "a yeirlie maill and deutie therefore" for what appears to be 60 “good dollars” a year for the term of his life, and one life thereafter. It also gives Robert Cheyne and his heirs planning permission “to big (build) ane hous and fortrice upon the saidis landis of Valay for sauftie thairof fra the Heland men,perattis and utheris invasionis”. Unlike modern planning permission, it does not say by when the works were to be done; in effect it was finally completed when Herbert Anderton finished his castellated Hall in 1900. About 100 years later we installed an old ships cannon on the terrace, trained on the west pier, to repel those “Heland men”. We did not apply for planning permission, relying on the original grant by King James in 1575.

Cannon on the terrace at Vaila Hall.
Richard Price supplies us with spare cannon balls from wrecks off Out Skerries.

In about 1582 Gorvel Faddersdotter surrendered her estates in Shetland to King Friderick of Denmark. On 26th March 1584 King James of Scotland wrote to King Friderick on behalf of Robert Cheyne, referring to his lease of Vaila, and asking King Friderick to respect his rights (FN7). In response to this on 18th October 1584 the King of Denmark gave a letter of tack (a lease) to Robert Cheyne of Vaila and Vaila "guidis" with confirmation from the King of Scotland, for a rent of 60 dollars per annum (then about 180 Scots pounds or 15 English pounds). (FN8).

This shows that 100 years after the annexation of Shetland, the Scots crown accepted ownership of the King of Denmark, which would have arisen under Udal law. On the other hand, Robert Cheyne was canny enough to get his lease recorded in Scotland, so keeping a boot in both Udal and Scots law.

A list of rental property acquired by the King of Denmark from Gorvel Faddersdottar on 25th August 1582 includes the item "Master Rubbert of Walo 24 marks of land, 8 pennies the mark, pays yearly 8 pund butter, 72 ells wattmell." (FN9). Thus the annual rent for Vaila was about 80 kg of butter (at 10 Kg per lispund) and about 150 feet of wadmell (coarse woven cloth at about 2 feet per cuttel). That's a lot of butter to keep fresh, and the weavers must have been kept busy on Vaila. The annual income of her total estate in Shetland was 136 punds of butter and 1120 ells of wadmell. You can work out how much that is in current weights and values.

The dispute between the Cheynes and the Hawiks over title to Vaila continued for the next 20 years with about half a dozen court hearings described as follows.

There was a hearing of the Court of Session in Edinburgh on 26th February 1584/5 where Robert Cheyne required Andrew Hawik to renounce this "right of title and kindness " to Vaila and other lands, and constitutes Robert Cheyne as assignee of wadsets (mortgages) of those lands granted by Andrew Hawik. (FN10).

The letter of tack to Robert Cheyne from the King of Denmark with confirmation from the King of Scotland was produced at a hearing on 29th July 1586 at Bruche before Earl Robert of Orkney, Lord of Yeitland in the on-going dispute between Robert Cheyne and Andrew Hawik over their rights to Vaila. Andrew Hawik produced no evidence although he had been the rent collector for Gorvel Faddersdottar, so Earl Robert ordered all "landmails" for the crop in 1586 and annually thereafter to Robert Cheyne. (FN11).

Robert Cheyne initiated another hearing before the Court of Session in Edinburgh on 14th March 1587/8 over payment of rent and duties from Vaila. In this action reference is made to an order by Earl Robert of Orkney on 2nd July 1585 that Robert Cheyne had the best right to the lands of Vaila and Vaila goods.

Robert Cheyne died in April 1591, and there is a further hearing before the Court of Session in Edinburgh on 4th February 1593/4 to decide on the competing claims of the Hawiks and Thomas Cheyne, son and heir of Robert Cheyne. The court heard that for 20 years the rents and duties had been paid to Robert Cheyne, and it held that Thomas Cheyne had the best right to the lands by virtue of the "gift and disposition made by Dame Gorvel Faddersdottar of Giske to the deceased Robert Cheyne for payment of an annual duty dated thursday after St Bartilmois Day 1572 and the ratification of the Regent dated 3rd March 1575/6". (FN12).

Nevertheless the Hawiks did not take this decision lying down, and evicted Thomas Cheyne and his tenants in Vaila on 7th December 1593, and despoiled their goods, as follows-

12 cows with calves at £10 each
5 oxen at 20 merks each
8 yelt nolt at 10 merks each
400 sheep (whereof 200 ewes) at £1 each
2 horses at £10 each
4 mares at £6 each
3 sows with grice at £3 each
2 iron pots at £2 each
2 copper kettles at £3 each
3 rouchs of bere, containing 20 bolls, at £4 per boll
12 reestit mutton boukis at £1 each
2 kists conatain 2 prs of sheets, 2prs blankets and 2 koddis at £10

The court ordered restoration of these goods (which had a total value of 685 Scots pounds), £20 for costs and £2 to the Lords collector. (FN13).

Interestingly the amount of animals supported by the Isle of Vaila then is remarkably similar to our own stocking rates. We have about 120 breeding ewes, 50 hogs and lambs, and four rams, 12 Highland cattle, five pigs and related piglets and six Shetland ponies. We have a few more sheets and duvets. If a koddis is a cot, we now have five, for my grandchildren and their friends. In fact a koddis is a pillow.

There was a hearing before the Sheriff's court in Scalloway on 30th July 1601 which heard the same evidence of Thomas Cheyne's title; the court confirmed his title and his right to the rents and duties.

The Sheriff Depute of Yetland, John Dischingtoun made an order entitling Thomas Cheyne to Vaila and Vaila guidis and ordered the Hawiks that they "nawis truble or molest the said Thomas."

On 6th September 1606 it was recorded that "on 10th August 1606 Andrew Vischert, bailyie of Waiss ... enterit and pooest Thomas Chein of Valay in the lands of Norby and all other lands and geir". And Eduard Scollay recorded Thomas Cheyne's entitlement to rents and duties for 1605, and in the future. (FN14). This appears to be the last recorded action between Thomas Cheyne and the Hawiks.

No doubt encouraged by his success, Thomas Cheyne continued to appear in the court at Scallowaybanks; the Court book of Shetland 1615-1629 describes about 20 such appearances in this period in a number of capacities. He was a member of the Assise, essentially a Grand Jury, a sutteris (a suitor), a cautioner (a surety), a receiver of oaths and a litigant in some half a dozen cases.

One of these related to claims by Andro Bruce that he was an assignee of a debt of "20 sufficient silver dollars" obtained while Thomas Cheyne was in Bergen. However Thomas produced a receipt for the debt and was exonerated. Maybe this was part of the annual rent for Vaila of 60 dollars payable to the King of Denmark.

The Scalloway court records ceased after Earl Patrick was removed in 1615 so we don't know what the litigious Cheynes were up to after that. However by 1664 it appears that they had acquired title to estates on the west-side of Shetland, including Foula and Vaila "through a labyrinthine series of grants, charters and mortgages, and by successfully playing off the Danish crown against the Scottish crown." (per John R Baldwin in Shetland's Northern Links- Language and History). But despite this, they were bankrupt by the end of the 17th century and Vaila had been wadsetted (mortgaged) to James Mitchell, a Scalloway merchant.

On 27th April 1697 Patrick Cheyne (presumably the son or grandson of Thomas Cheyne) transferred his lands on Vaila comprising 21 merks and 3 merks at Cloudin to this James Mitchell of Girlsta. (FN15). A copy of the conveyance, together with a number of mortgages and related documents are in the Shetland Archive. James Mitchell built the old Ha at Vaila; the Mitchell family crest appears above the old front door on the north side of the old Ha dated 1696; and also at the entrance to the north court-yard.

Before his death in 1743 James Mitchell transferred his estates in Shetland to his grandson, John Scott of Melby, son of his daughter Grizel, and John Scott of Gibblesdon, Fife, on 14th January 1736. These included the islands of Foula and Vaila, and lands of Melby, Footabrough and Sandness , namely 465 merks in the parish of Walls and Sandness, and 8 merks in Gaiderhouse in Aithsting. A merk was a description of an area of land, by reference to its value, rather than its size. Thus say two acres of poor land equal in value to one acre of good land, could each be called a merk.

This John Scott of Melby (died 1765) was known as Old Melby; there are many stories of this "scheming, violent-tempered, but not altogether unkindly old tyrant" (per I. B. Stoughton Holbourn in the Isle of Foula). He settled in the old Ha at Vaila.

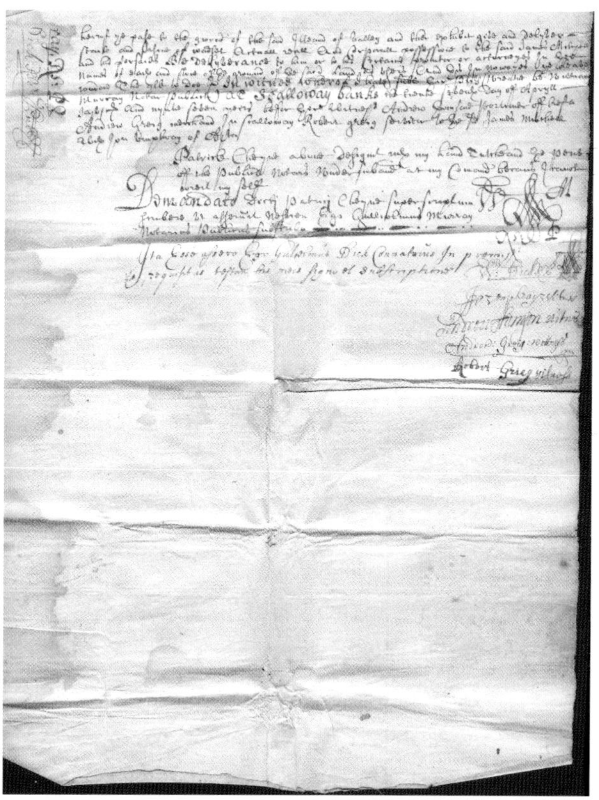

Copy Conveyance of Vaila from Patrick Cheyne to James Mitchell dated 27th April 1697. (Shetland Archive)

His son John Scott (1737-1764) received a disposition of Vaila from Old Melby on 7th July 1756, but when he died young in 1764 the estate passed to his son, another John Scott (1760-1850). His son, yet another John Scott (1782-1813) died in the wreck of the Doris in Cruden Bay. His son also John Scott (1804-1850) had no children. But a second son Robert Thomas Charles (1812-1875) succeeded him at last breaking the chain of John Scotts. He is recorded in the census of 1871 as then living at Melby House, Sandness with his wife, two children and four domestics; he was the General Inspector of the Hospital to the Fleet and

Deputy Lieutenant of Orkney and Zetland. His first son, not surprisingly was also called Robert Thomas Charles (born 1864). And his son (born 1885) had the same name.

Thus in the history of ownership of Vaila there were five John Scotts and two Robert Thomas Charles Scotts; they were an imaginative bunch in their choice of names.

The 19th century census records show that the Scotts chose Melby House, Sandness as their residence, rather than Vaila, although when Edward Charlton visited Vaila in 1832, he was royally entertained there by the last John Scott. (See Chapter 7). When Charlton returned in 1852, he learnt of John Scott's death from the factor.

In 1837 Arthur Anderson, the founder of the P&O Shipping company leased Vaila from the Scotts and established the Shetland Fishing Company there. This contributed to breaking the power of the lairds who had previously controlled all fishing by their tenants.

Under this system, the laird supplied all the equipment, boats and nets, but kept the catch only allowing the tenant fishermen to keep the heads and tails. The laird paid for the fish by the provision of food and general supplies. This Truck or barter system was akin to slavery and was not abolished until the Truck Acts in the 19th century. Anderson's company allowed tenants to fish outside this system. He also tried new ways of curing fish on pallets. His operation on Vaila can be seen in a contemporary painting, a copy of which hangs in our kitchen. The original is in the Shetland Museum. The fishing company ceased operations after a few years.

By this time Vaila was supporting a number of tenant crofter/fishermen. With the increase of blanket peat the improved areas for farming were limited, and the worstening weather would have made arable farming difficult. The 1881 census records James Laurenson as farming 640 acres,18 arable on Vaila. The tenants would have relied more and more on fishing, and possibly catching sea birds. Old Melby had built Mucklaberry Tower at the entrance to Wester Sound in the 18th century; originally with a sloping roof. One of its uses

Contemporary picture of Vaila showing the operations of Arthur Anderson's Shetland Fishing Company in 1837. (Shetland Museum)

may have been to watch out over the tenants' fishing operations to check that they were not landing their catch secretly to avoid giving it to the laird. It might also have been used as a look out for excise men by smugglers shipping in contraband.

Mucklaberry Tower, before renovation and castellation by Herbert Anderton. (Shetland Museum)

By 1873 the land and sea were insufficient to support the tenants on Vaila, which was described as the largest farm in Shetland occupied by fishermen. An article from *The Shetland Times* describing their emigration to New Zealand is in Chapter 7.

The census records from 1841 show the shifts in population of Vaila over this period; there were 29 in 1841, comprising a number of households, probably some of whom carried on the Shetland Fishing Company. By 1861 there were 17 and ten years later just 11, the family of Magnus and Marion Thomson, with six of overall nine sons, who would have emigrated in 1873. By 1891 numbers had increased to 19, comprising two households also of Thomsons.

Herbert Anderton, a wealthy Bradford mill owner, used to visit Shetland for fishing and shooting holidays, and to buy wool for his mills. During a visit he was entranced by the scenery and resolved to buy an island. Foula was then being auctioned and he instructed an agent to bid for him. But the story goes that the agent over-indulged at lunch and missed the auction. Instead Herbert made do with Vaila and some 10,000 acres on the west-side which he acquired in 1888. Foula was sold at the same time to Ewing Gilmour, and then to I. B. Stoughton Holbourn in 1900.

The Old Ha, Vaila, in 1890. (Shetland Museum)

Herbert immediately set about a major re-construction programme similar to that of the Bullough's on Rum, restoring the old Ha with a Victorian conservatory and garden with an elaborate fountain. He built the boat house at Ham which doubled as an artists studio,

The conservatory and castellated out-house were Herbert Anderton's first additions to Vaila Hall. (Shetland Museum)

primarily for his brother Francis Swithin Anderton and also to house his collection of far eastern artefacts. It gained notoriety as a Buddist temple and was known locally as " the House of Gods".

Oriental artefacts in the Buddhist Temple at Ham. (Shetland Museum)

In 1894 the farmhouse at Cloudin was built in the Arts and Crafts style with crow-stepped roofs. He acquired a stock of Shetland ponies from the Duke of Londonderry's stud in Bressay, as well as a herd of Jersey cows for milk.

Alison Harper "Cloudin", 2008, watercolour, 10½ x 7½ inches.

He then turned his attention to the Hall; he engaged architect E.P.Peterson of Bradford to design his baronial hall. It made use of the old Ha as the south wing, and farm buildings opposite the old front door on the north side to create a "nouveau riche" wing, with the Great Hall in between.

Outside there are battlements, pepper pot towers with corbelling in the style of those at Muness and Scalloway castles and a large circular bell tower in the north west corner. The east end of the 40 foot high Great Hall, with a carved red Moroccan mahogany ceiling has large stained glass windows depicting the Anderton crest; this includes sets of shackles and the stained glass includes a cheerful black face. You can draw your own conclusions. The west end houses a stone-clad minstrels gallery with excellent acoustics. We have introduced a large brass "eagle" lecturn there for impromptu readings and sermons.

Although the morning sun provides good light through the stained glass windows, the lack of any other windows makes the Great Hall a gloomy place for the rest of the day. Herbert installed white canvass on the floor to reflect as much light as possible.

The building of the Hall can be seen from contemporary photos. The rubble and sandstone would have been obtained locally. But the carved and dressed sandstone for the

The building of the Great Hall between the Old Ha and the "nouveau riche wing". (Shetland Museum)

Vaila Hall about 1900 after restoration by Herbert Anderton. (Shetland Museum)

crenellations, turrets, and the supporting arches for the minstrels gallery and the fire-place were prepared in Yorkshire and shipped up to Vaila.

By 1900 the building was complete and the interior was furnished in the Victorian-Jacobean style. There were red velvet chairs, a 20ft mahagony table, black stained wood Jacobean revival cabinets, corner cupboards, and settle and a fine oak refectory table. At the east end of the Great Hall stood two 10ft long raised settles, for viewing billiards, which we have restored in their original green leather. There are a similar ones in the Durbar room at Osborne House on the Isle of Wight. The massive semi-circular fireplace was hung with pikes and ancient muskets; armorial shields and cavalry swords adorned the minstrels gallery, and Herbert's family portraits decked the walls. Photographs from Henry Anderton's guide book in 1971 show how little the Great Hall had changed from its original state. It is like a time warp, and we have preserved the no-change policy. The only significant change has been the removal of the "Munsters" from the walls; these have of course been retained by Henry. We have also introduced a suit of costume armour which we felt was missing.

Herbert also built a boat house at Ham; here the architects only came up with a variant on those commonly seen on the Thames, with a wooden balcony for relaxing or carousing. We found a number of old black bottles by the pier below the boathouse; an easy bottle throw away.

The boat house at Ham. (Shetland Museum)

As befits an island laird, Herbert had a fine teak launch built in 1898 by John Samuel White at East Cowes, Isle of Wight and shipped up to Vaila. She was about 30 feet long and powered by a steam engine with an imposing funnel, with leather backed seats for passengers around the gunwale and a canvas roof for weather protection. She would have been too delicate to leave out on the trot-line in the harbour at Ham, so instead she was housed in the boat house; but every morning she was winched into the water, and the steam engine fired up in case the laird wanted to go for a spin. The boatman lived in a shed

Herbert Anderton's teak launch in about 1900. (Shetland Museum)

on the pier. She was known as "the Teak launch". Tommy Moncrieff bought her from Miss Foster, installing a cabin and a diesel engine; Jimmy Moncrieff remembers a trip to Norway in her.

In 1995, Phillip's held an auction of Traditional River Craft and Ephemera at Henley including the much restored teak launch. (See extract from the sale particulars in Chapter 7). The boat looked amazing moored by the towing path; a rare Simpson, Strickland steam engine replaced the diesel engine, reflecting in her highly polished mahogany wood-work; the striped canvas cover shaded the beautiful burgundy leather seats from the midday sun. We bid up to £35,000 but were out-bid. It would have been wonderful to have re-united her with her original home at Ham; but in reality she would have had little use and her varnished wooden hull would have been a prey to Shetland conditions. Nor would she have had a full time crew living in the shed at Ham. She is probably happier taking jolly crowds of mashers in striped blazers and boaters, and their ladies to cheer on the oarsmen at Henley.

Next to the harbour at Ham lie gardens developed by Herbert, about four acres overall, of which about one acre is walled and thus able to support the cultivation of a number of plants and flowers. There are a number of sycamore trees, which grow to just above the height of the surrounding walls, as well as dense thickets of roses and escalonia. Each year Jill Slee Blackadder has organised a "garden party" of keen gardeners to tend the gardens, and plant, cultivate and encourage growth of a number of locally cultivated Shetland plants.

Herbert is buried in the garden, with a headstone donated by his grateful tenants, as is his sister Florence Ruth Foster, who inherited the estate from him in 1937. She had married Col Foster, another mill owner, who had acquired Burrastow House nearby. She died in 1953, and the estate passed to their daughter Gwendoline Ruth Foster who suffered from multiple sclerosis. She died in 1969, leaving the estate to Henry. She is also buried at Ham, as are Henry's father's ashes. Dorota has also booked a space there, to be with her beloved bulldog Nosek and Great Dane Effie.

Herbert Anderton entertains his guests; note the lady trying to get a signal on her mobile phone. (Shetland Museum)

The first decade of the 20th century would have seen many lavish house parties at Vaila, which Herbert used as a summer residence. The 1901 census shows 15 people living on Vaila. A cook and house-maid in the Hall, and two households of those ubiquitous Thomsons. In 1901 30 people worked on the island, including a staff of eight in the hall, three roadmen and several shepherds, gardeners, grooms, and that lonely boatman at Ham. One maid's job was to continually feed the peat fires around the house, like re-painting the Firth of Forth Bridge. Herbert set up the Walls Regatta Club, donating the Vaila Cup for an annual yacht race around Vaila. He also sponsored many public works in

Drawing prepared by E. P. Peterson of Bradford for Herbert Anderton for an additional wing to Vaila Hall.

Walls and in 1915 was developing plans for a village institute there, designed by his Bradford architects to ressemble a cricket pavilion, a chapel on Vaila to seat a congregation of 100 and to extend the Hall by the addition of a servants wing to the east of the kitchen, and a courtyard beyond it.

The on-set of the First World War put an end to all these grandiose plans. Henry's father who was about ten at that time remembered staying at Vaila, where he used to run around the tops of the 8ft high stone walls in the garden. When the declaration of war was announced the family had to leave Shetland and the Hall immediately. During one of his last visits to Vaila, he ran along most of the garden wall, much to his son's horror.

The war also saw an end to Herbert's lavish house parties. The textile market was uncertain, and when he tried to keep his mills going during the slump, he lost his fortune. He retired to Vaila in 1933, living in virtual isolation, supported by two devoted servants from Yorkshire until his death in 1937.

So in this quickly sketched time line of Vaila the early settlers were in residence for some 3,000/4,000 years, followed possibly by more "early English" in the 5th century AD. Then there was Norse settlement from the 9th century to the 15th century, until the end of the ownership of the "Lords of Norway". The Cheynes became the new Scottish owners in the 17th century, but had to sell after 100 years tenure. The Mitchells then built the old Ha and title passed by descent through seven generations of Scotts, for 200 years until the sale to Herbert Anderton in 1888. The Andertons' reign lasted 100 years until 1993. At the time of writing we have been here a mere 15 years.

Chapter 5

Flora and Fauna

I have never been much good on flowers. Early training from "When we were six" by A A Milne taught me the difference between Geraniums red and Delphiniums blue, and apart from a passing interest in growing Lobelias in my window box in my parent's flat in Earls Court, that is about it. So writing a chapter on Flora on Vaila is a challenge.

I have however learnt a bit about Shetland flora. Most of the plants are small, wild and the growing season very short. Spring, summer and autumn are compressed into June to August. But the colours, pinks, blues and yellows are vibrant, and the whole amounts to a hands down victory to nature over climate.

Of course the fauna can take its toll on the flora. Henry had a lot of sheep who had the run of the island for a number of years. At least we had a clean slate to start on.

The house has some three separate walled gardens. Hamish Thomson (who was not related to the Shetland Thomsons) re-designed two with curved lawns and a lily pond. We removed the remains of Herbert's elaborate fountain with putti to improve the lawn for croquet. Stevie Jay took over as Head of Gardening in 1999 and has expanded the policy of concentrating on local species. Curiously he has a degree in Forestry, but chooses to live in a virtually treeless landscape. Hopefully some of the several thousand saplings planted on Vaila will bear fruit.

Stevie's main aim has been to limit maintenance and encourage growth of anything that wants to grow here. For example, Rosa Ragosa, Fuchsia, Red Hot Pokers, Euphorbia, Lingularea, Gunnera and Hostas; and Willows from Lapland, Iceland and Alaska. He is slightly defensive when pointing out that the upper gardens are more exposed than other

Shetland gardens. He notes stoically that the gardens were completely destroyed in a 30 minute summer storm on 13th June 2001.

Herbert also developed some extensive gardens at Ham within a walled area, essential for protection from the wind. There were dense thickets of stumpy Sycamores and Escalonias, so the whole effect was that of a secret garden, lost in time. The Sycamores are over 100 years old, but no more than 16ft high. Hamish, Stevie and Jill Slee Blackadder's team have transformed this area, training the Escalonias and Salmonberry and using the cover provided by the Sycamores to re-stock the gardens. On a quiet day, the gardens at Ham are like another world.

Top: Olga on the croquet lawn with background water feature.

Middle: Author's favourite gunnera.

Bottom: Sunken garden from the battlements.

Gardens at Ham.

I am surprised that the main development of Vaila was around the West Pier, rather than at Ham; maybe the well sheltered harbour there was not deep enough.

Also near the house are two extensive kitchen gardens, no doubt fully operational when there was an army of gardeners. One is now used as a nursery for conditioning saplings to Shetland weather. The other is now well developed, with healthy tree cover, and produces

Gardens at Ham.

prize winning entries of potatoes, carrots, onions, beetroot and leeks at the Walls annual agricultural show at the end of the first week in August. Unfortunately we can't eat our produce until then. We don't use poly-tunnels, but when we were re-constructing our potting shed we found that the glazier had supplied double glazing. He must have thought that nothing was too good for those struggling plants on Vaila.

Kery Dalby is a regular summer visitor; a leading lichenologist he with his wife Claire has written the seminal text on Shetland lichens. I have learnt that lichens range from being so common that we don't really "see" them; even the "grey" on rocks is often lichen rather than stone, to being inaccessible even to lichenologists, which must be rather frustrating for them. Vaila has a wide assortment; Kery is always looking for a new species here which will rock the world of lichenologists.

Grey and yellow lichens on the rocks at Maamy's Hole.

We don’t have rabbits, stoats, poll cats, rats or mice. So nesting birds only have to cope with otters (about three sets) and some hedgehogs introduced in Henry’s time to eat slugs on the hostas and strawberries.

Over the years, the bird population fluctuates. At one stage the Great Skuas were harrowing the Kittiwakes, and possibly the Terns. The Great Skuas have not breed on Vaila for two years before this year, so the Terns are making a come-back. But the Great Skuas are breeding this year and protecting their nests fiercely.

The most consistent residents are the Fulmars, nesting on the rock ledges, and soaring effortlessly on thermals. We see occasional Puffins and the usual array of gulls, including pairs of large Black Backed gulls, the scourge of unprotected lambs, and many Shags on the offshore stacks, hanging out their wings to dry. We have regular pairs of Red Throated Divers nesting on our main lochan and many “estuary” birds, Curlews, Snipe and Whimbrel. My favourites are the Oyster Catchers, waddling around like grumpy old couples.

It occurs to me that the name of Vaila, based on Val-øy, falcon isle, could now be replaced by Great Skua or Bonxie Isle.

Chapter 6

Images of Vaila

Our earliest image is the painting done in about 1837 showing Arthur Anderson's Vaila Fishing Company in full operation. (see Chapter 4). The original was in the Bod of Gremista in Lerwick where he was brought up. It shows the old Ha and cottages around the West Pier, fish drying on pallets near the burnt mound, and fishing smacks at anchor in Vaila Voe. Despite a little artistic licence with some of the contours, little has changed. There are even two figures in the foreground redolent of seafarers' yarns as in the style of the Childhood of Raleigh. The original is now in the Shetland Museum.

Claire Dalby RWS, RE, comes each summer; her highly personal style of watercolour, with hundreds of worked lines, is well adapted to the scenary and skies of Vaila. She is no colourist, but her subtle tones and enormous application create works of great beauty.

Claire Dalby RWS, RE, "Tower on Vaila with Foula", 2006, watercolour, 11⅛ x 8 inches.

Claire Dalby RWS, RE, "Vaila's Tower from the North", 2005, watercolour, 11⅝ x 8⅛ inches.

David Severn from Beeston, Notts who now lives in Tokyo, has visited us on a number of occasions. His artistic imagination is vast; rather than wedding photographs, we commissioned him to do a picture depicting our guests in the various circus related costumes in which they came. We had a clutch of clowns, ring masters and dare-devils fired from cannons in goggles and Y fronts. Our watch-tower appears in his Ancestral Lynx, but he has rather overdone the trees.

David Severn "Ancestra Lynx", 1994, mixed media on paper, 26½ x 16⅝ inches.

David Severn "Wedding Portrait Panorama", 1994, mixed media on paper, 29½ x 18⅝ inches.

From our early days my mother loved coming to sketch and enjoy the scenery. We would install her in the Land Rover in remote locations to work on her landscape paintings, primarily watercolours. One day we forgot to retrieve her, but she took it well. Her pictures are well observed, executed in control of her medium, and very easy on the eye.

Joyce Rowland "The Watchtower from Vaila Hall", watercolour, 11½ x 8½ inches.

Joyce Rowland
"Conservatory interior, Vaila Hall",
watercolour, 8½ x 11⅛ inches.

In July 2007, Tony Bream came for a few weeks to do a Shetland series, and a number of drawings of me. (see frontispiece). A real out-door pleine-aire painter, he concentrated on views around the Watchtower, working in oils with massive brushes and wide sweeps of colour, yet depicting his subjects with style, panache and with great visual impact.

Antony Bream "Maamy's Hole", 2007, oil on canvas on board.

Antony Bream "Nouns Geo, Isle of Vaila", oil on canvas on board, 15½ x 13⅝ inches.

Antony Bream "Interior Great Hall, Vaila Hall", 2007, oil on canvas, 16 x 22 inches.

In 2003 Caroline MacAdam Clark RWS was visiting friends in Shetland and came to stay a few days on the island. Her very individual style shows seascapes on hazy summer days, with beams of light dazzling your vision. Not many days in Shetland are like this, but her pictures are the stuff of whimsy and nostalgia.

Caroline MacAdam Clark RWS. "Foula, the Edge of the World", 2003, oil and pencil on board, 20½ x 8½ inches.

Ron Sandford, a draughtsman with a truly individual and committed style came to live in Yell in 2002. He and his wife Meilo, a well established book illustrator don't drive and have a wheel-barrow to cart stuff from the bus to their croft, so take their isolation seriously. By comparison we are like butterflies, flitting from place to place. The rocky coast of Vaila is the perfect subject for his highly stylised approach to rocks, pebbles,and any thing similar, of which there is a lot in Shetland!

Ron Sandford, "View west from Quoy Hill, Isle of Vaila", pen and watercolour wash, 28½ x 21½ inches.

His friend and driver, Mike McDonnell produces quirky bas-reliefs; his Bird Tariff has pride of place in the Watchtower.

Mike McDonnell, "Bird Tariff", wooden construction, 18½ x 25⅞ inches.

Richard Rowland, "Vaila Hall", etching, aquatint, 7½ x 5⅞ inches.

I realised fairly early after coming here that Shetland is the ideal foil for the luminosity and contrast of my black and white aquatints. I have now done about 35 Shetland etchings, some of Vaila being those shown here.

Richard Rowland, "Wester Sound from Vaila Hall", etching, aquatint, 15 x 9⅝ inches.

Didier Piquer is a photographer from Paris who enjoys capturing the changing moods of Shetland, as in his book Sips of Shetland. His splendid dramatic photograph of Vaila from Burrastow appears as the frontispiece to this book.

Finally, I have included a wistful photograph of Vaila as it was before we came, from The Shetland Story by Liv Kjorsvik Schei with photographs by Gunnie Moberg. Gunnie died last year having made her home in Orkney for many years, and becoming one of the best known and loved photographers of the Northern Isles.

Vaila Hall in the 1980s (Gunnie Moberg). She brought George Mackay Brown to Vaila as described in Chapter 7.

Chapter 7

A Vaila Miscellany

The main aim of this book was to assemble a number of writings, photos and illustrations of Vaila in one place. Apart from Henry Anderton's short guide-book in 1971 there have been no works dedicated to Vaila.

As mentioned in Chapter 3 (Early Settlement), the Welsh monk, Nennius recorded Hengist and Horsa's visit to Orkney in 443 A.D. Here is a translation of the text taken from the Early English Settlement of Orkney and Shetland by Graeme Davis.

> *"Hengist ... said to Vortigern, "... I will send you my son and his brother, both valiant men, who at my invitation will fight against the Picts, and you can give them the countries in the north, near the wall called Gual." The incautious sovereign having assented to this, Octa and Ebusa arrived with forty ships. In these they sailed round the country of the Picts, laid waste the Orkneys, and took possession of many regions, even to the Pictish confine beyond the Frenesic sea."*

In Chapter 1 (The Isle of Vaila), I mentioned the Ballad of Hildina, a major surviving text in Orkney and Shetland Norn. Graeme Davis has written an interesting critique of this "folk-ballad" and has also produced a new English translation as follows.

> *"Once upon a time the Earl of Orkney asked his brother*
> *'From out her glass pavilion should I steal our King's daughter?'*
> *'My brother if you take this maiden from her glass pavilion*
> *Your deed will be remembered for years a million million.'*

Thus when the King came home from Viking voyage a winner
The stepmother was still at home, but there was no Hildina.
'I swear that by all that's holy that wherever he may be
I'll hang him by his neck from the highest tree.'

To good St Magnus' Church in Orkney fled the Earl,
To Orkney sped the King, to save his little girl.
Meeting the married lady there he boxed her round the ears
Soon down her white cheeks there flowed a flood of tears.
The Earl embraced Hildina and kissed her on the cheek,
'My darling wife, between us two, whose death would you now seek?'
'Not to my father but to you I swore my lasting vow,
And so by that we both may rule, us two in Orkney now.'

'Go to you horse and overtake my father on the beach
Greet him kindly, clasp hands, his blessing to beseech.'
The King made a stern reply, his anger did not falter,
'I want to know what bride price you can give me for my daughter?'
'Thirty marks of burnished gold shall I unto you give,
And you will never lack a son as long as I may live.'
Long stood the King, gazed on the Earl for long,
'You're worth a thousand sons my man, though what you did was wrong.'

Now among the King's companions was the swarthy Hiluge,
To wed the beauteous Hildina his dream for many a day.
Again and again and craftily Hiluge spoke to the King,
Again and again the King did listen, once more to this thing.
Now for a long time the King looked at the Earl standing near
'You may not, Orkney; a long time ago I betrothed my daughter dear.'
"I will take nothing against his will from the King your father,
Instead to give Hiluge his rights, that I would rather.'

Hildina looked from one to the other, turning pale,
One would die in the fight, that fate would not fail.
Now the earl stepped forward onto the duelling ground
and the King turned his face from Orkney, looked around.
'Now one of us must die, 'tis either thee or me.'
The blows rained down, down fell the Earl of Orkney.
Now Lady Hildina steps on to the grass where soon a corpse must lie,
'Father by all that's holy do not let a brave man die.'

But Hiluge answered her; 'Call Odin's maidens here,
For death draws nigh the Earl, this man your husband dear'.
Now the earl felt the axe bite through his neck, a clean kill
Hiluge threw the head into her arms; she grew more angry still.
'You promised me marriage if I voyaged far from our land
Now with golden dowry and strong vows give me Hildina's hand.'
Now were her eyes downcast as she looked upon the King
For the Lady Hildina against her will must take a golden ring.

Soon that time came, though Hildina wished it never,
With that man to be joined, husband and wife forever.
Now Hildina asked her father 'May I serve the wine,
choose who will get the best, who the worst, when we come to dine?'
'Both the best and the worst as you think,
Both earls and freemen this day must drink.'
A drugged wine she gave them, both to earls and to freemen,
Their eyes were heavy, sleep soon came over them.

Then the Lady Hildina went in, her face was set,
She saw her father and the guests asleep, on the benches where they sat.
Then the Lady Hildina went in, dragged her father across the floor,
Laid him on the grass outside and fastened close the door.

Now Hiluge awakes as the fire begins to rage,
The smoke is black and thick, the banquets hall a cage.
Now a scream breaks from the throat of Hiluge,
'Oh Lady Hildina, let me live another day.'

'So may you cry out, now you should believe,
That same mercy you showed in the battle, now you shall receive,
You did not care for him or me, that was clear for all to see,
Then you threw his head at me, that angered me.
Now receive a heavy fate, for soon to death you yield,
The King cannot help you know, on this battlefield.'
All this for once upon a time the earl of Orkney asked his brother
'From out her glass pavilion should I steal our King's daughter?' "

In 1832 Edward Charlton toured Shetland and after a visit to Vaila, sailed to Foula where he learnt that an old man named William Hendrie, living on Foula, was then the only remaining Shetlander who could recite the Ballad of Hildina in Orkney and Shetland Norn

George Low visited Shetland and made notes of his travels in 1774. They were published in 1879 entitled "A Tour through the Islands of Orkney and Shetland: containing Hints relative to their Ancient, Modern and Natural History collected in 1774."

He recorded examples of Orkney and Shetland Norn; an example, known as the Cunningsburgh Phrase (shown in Graeme Davis' book) is as follows.

"Myrk in e liora	*It is dark in the chimney*
Luce in e liunga	*There is light on the heather*
Timin e guest in	*It is time for the guest inside*
Eeeee geungna!	*OUT should go!"*

This bears remarkable similarities with a number of Polish folk ballads which Dorota sings in the style of Jeremy Hardy. One such is as follows.

"Jada goście jada
Od samego Gdańska
A do mmie nie jada
Bo ja tu nie miszkom
Oj dana!"

She has translated this.

"Guests are coming
All the way from Gdansk.
But they won't see me
Because I don't live here.
Hey!"

The last text in Orkney and Shetland Norn was recorded in Foula by George Isbister in 1958, (again from Graeme Davis' book) as follows.

From the Eagle Song

"Ante pedu, sat a growla
Sat a growla festa
Pirla moga, hench a boga
Settar alla nesta"

My extempore "translation" of this is.

"Once there sat a fierce dog
Before going for a pee
The cat did a purler, and fell in the bog
And the eagle to its nest did flee"

One well recorded Vaila superstition relates to cats, which cannot abide living on Vaila. This was recounted by the Rev. John Brand in "A new description of Orkney, Zetland, Pightland-Firth and Caithness" (1703) and has been reproduced in County Folklore Vol VII Orkney and Shetland Islands, collected by G.F. Black 1903 as follows.

"Vaila. There is a little Isle on the West side of Waes called Vaila, wherin there is no cat, neither will any stay tho brought in, as hath been done for trial, but will quickly be gone, they either dying or betaking themselves to Sea, they endeavour to sweem to the next Isle; Yet about 50 Years ago there was one seen

upon this Isle, about that time when a Gentleman the Proprietor thereof was Tormented and put to death by the Witches, but never any were seen since, save what were brought in for trial, as now said. The reason of this I could not learn from the Ministers, who gave the information, it is like because of the Air, or the smell of something upon the Isle, tho not perceivable by the Inhabitants, which agreeth not with the temper and Constitution of these animals."

In 1900 I.B. Stoughton Holbourn bought the Isle of Foula from Ewing Gilmour. He collected a number of stories about Foula, and Vaila, and these were published after his death in 1938. Here are extracts from this book, The Isle of Foula, which relate to Vaila.

"About this time (1720) the island (Foula), as well as the estate of Melby, Vaila and other lands, was owned by James Mitchell of Girlesta and his daughter and co-heir Grizel, who married John Scott of Gibblesdon, grandson of Sir John Scott of Scotstarvet (an author who had a seat in the Privy Council in 1617 and was Lord of Session in 1649) and Anne, daughter of Sir John Drummond of Hawthorn Den. Through Grizel the property was settled on her son John Scott (of whom there were nine in succession, which is apt to confuse the most accurate memory), [in fact there were five John Scotts and two Robert Thomas Charles Scotts; see Chapter 4] and it was he who is known in Foula as Old Melby; and many are the tales that are told of this scheming, violent- tempered, but not altogether unkindly old tyrant."

"The Scotts settled in the island of Vaila, where they built what is known as the Old Ha', and as Vaila lies just opposite Ham Voe [on Foula] they changed their landing place and abandoned the south landing [on Foula] which the Danes had always used ...".

"In Vaila, Melby kept a muckle dog to frighten the folk who came to complain of ill-treatment. He said he was "tired of people speering at his lug," so built a great wall with two high gates between the house and the kitchen which, as was

the custom in those days, was a separate building. Someone who had the welfare of people at heart warned him that he could shut out the voice of man but not the voice of conscience. When a critic remarked that the wind would blow down the gates, he replied that he defied all the powers in hell to take down his yetts. One night a mysterious inscription appeared on the banks below his house. It was in foreign characters-Greek or Hebrew-so he sent to Lerwick for an interpreter. The translation ran, YOU ARE ALL IN POMP AND GRANDEUR NOW BUT MARK THE LATTER END. That night, although it was calm and still, the walls and gates fell down with a mighty roar like thunder. Many saw therein the hand of Providence, but there were others who stated that a strange ship had been sailing below the house, and they suggested that a charge of gunpowder had something to do with it."

"Old Melby built the lighthouse which is still to be seen on Vaila, and one day when his son, who went every where on horseback, was riding out to look at it both he and his pony fell over the cliffs and were lost. He left a little boy, an infant in his mother's arms. About the same year Melby lost a third wife ...".

"The following year he himself died, leaving the burden of the heavily mortgaged estate on the shoulders of the little four-year-old grandson. His guardians thought of selling the property but he was such a pretty child that they resolved to hold on and give him the chance to redeem it. Every now and again a summons would come for his father's and grandfather's debt, and they would solemnly place the missive in the little boy's hands. Nor did he disappoint them, for when he grew up he bought fish and sent it to Spain, and made sufficient money to clear the estate."

George Low also visited Vaila on 30th June 1774, describing his visit as follows.

"Landed at Vaila, an island in the mouth of Grueting-voe, which it serves to cover from westerly winds, and stretching along forms the excellent harbour of

Lingasound. Vaila is more than a mile long, almost oval, surrounded on the sea-side with high rocks, tho' little inhabited by birds. The human inhabitants consist of six families, who cultivate a small spot on the north end of the island. Here is a modern house and gardens belonging to Scott of Melbie, the proprietor, with a booth and every material for curing fish, many thousands of which are dried here annually for export. At this time the beach was covered with Cod, Tusk and Ling, which are the only marketable fish ..."

"Common Bear grows here with such luxuriancy that even at this season it was beginning to lodge, but in a good measure this was owing to the long continued rains of the season. All kinds of grain are here ready to sea-gust, owing to the high rocks which surround the coasts and throw the spray amongst the fields; and if this happens while the corns are green or in flower, spoils the crop for the year. It was formerly said no cat would live on Vaila; however this has been found a mistake, as mice have been some time ago introduced and thrive notably, so that the former are now become necessary."

"A great deal of bog Iron in the mosses of Vaila. The country people dye a sort of black with the mossy earth and water, which is much impregnated with it"

"Great quantities of the Rhodiola rosea in the rocks, as also the Ligusticium Scoticum."

In 1832 Edward Charlton was entertained on Vaila by John Scott. In his travel journal, Travels in Shetland 1832-1852 published in 2008 by his grandson, he rather confuses the age of this John Scott with his father who lived to 91 years; certainly he was royally entertained. Extracts from his journal are as follows.

"We soon bargained for a boat to Vailley, and having dismissed our crew of porters with the quantity of a shilling a head, we descended to the shore, and

were soon on a most beautiful summer's eve gliding over the smooth waters of the voe ..."

Edward Charlton describes his adventures birding on the southern cliffs of Vaila; you will have to read that in the original book. He then describes another feast.

"Even at this season Mr Scott could furnish a repast worthy of a southern table. Fish in the summer is the most plentiful article of food, and today we had tusk, ling, cod, all fresh and admirably cooked, for a Shetland chef de cuisine piques himself not a little on the various modes of dressing the finny inhabitants of the ocean. Mutton, smoked beef and vegetables succeeded, and then to our surprise appeared a monstrous pudding, flanked by a bowl of thick, luscious cream that no hermit could resist. To this succeeded cheese, to that tea and toast, and an hour or so after came a copious supper, followed by sundry libations of brandy, rum, whisky or gin until at length we escaped to rest."

I am pleased to report that Dorota works hard to keep up these standards of catering on Vaila.

As mentioned in Chapter 4, there was a mass exodus of tenants from Vaila in 1873 as described in the Shetland Times of 5th May 1873.

Walls

"There are several families in the quarter about to leave for New Zealand. The tenants of the island of Vaila, the largest farm in Shetland occupied by fishermen, are amongst the number. Here many of the crofts are too small, and would require two or three of them put together before there can be much agricultural improvement. Keyshies, spades, timmer shouls, wooden teethed harrows and heather besoms for "swooping" in the seed, are out of date. We Zetch would not wish a single eviction made for vile Scottish improvement, but lairds, as tacks become vacant and families emigrate, should unite crofts for we are overpeopled. It was the interest in days gone past of fishcuring landlords to multiply outsets

and divide tacks into half-tacks and quarter-tacks, but those days, we hope, are gone for ever."

In the 1880's George Sands was living on Foula and Vaila. He was highly critical of the barter or truck system which kept the crofters in penury on Foula. Here is poem he wrote about it (which appears in the Isle of Foula by I.B. Stoughton Holbourn).

"In Vaila Isle I now reside,
A pleasant dwelling place to me,
And far across the azure tide,
The peaks o' Foula I can see,
Which seem to me to say whene'er I look
"Perform the task you undertook."

In all our houses you have been,
You ate our bread, you shared our cup,
Our joys and sorrows you have seen,
You know the wound we cover up.
Oh! Speak for us; we dare not speak
Lest those in power their vengeance wreak

Put not your trust in parliament;
Many may suffer e'er it save;
But shout until the heavens are rent
That Foula sits a fettered slave
Chained to the oar and kept in tears,
While "Truck," the pirate, domineers."

George Sands also wrote a poem about Vaila, quoted by *The Shetland Times* (and also appearing in the Isle of Foula by I.B. Stoughton Holbourn). It was originally printed in "King James' Wedding and other Rhymes" and published by J. Bunhle, Arbroath, 1888, and this is the version shown below, except I have included some additional verses from the Isle of Foula version. The poem refers to Christie Thomson, as aged 88, which was in 1884, which dates the poem from then. It goes on a bit, but we support its sentiment.

Vaila

The rain it raineth every day,
Varied by gales with hail and spray,
Small pleasure now it is to stray
Upon the cliffs of Vaila.

Come let me paint in homely style
A picture of this little isle,
In length and breadth about a mile
Yet large enough is Vaila.

The South and West confront the deep,
And there the crags are high and steep,
Yet broken billows often leap,
Above the rocks of Vaila.

And when the wintry tempests blow
The sea breaks on the stacks like snow,
And yeasty froth fills every geo
Around the coast of Vaila.

Then spin-drift mingles with the air,
And all the ground is wet and bare,
And quadrupeds but poorly fare
For many months in Vaila.

The shaggy ponies, lean and weak,
The pebbly beach for sea-weed seek,
And crunching tangles in their cheek
Support their lives in Vaila.

Within a manor house I dwell,
Erected, as escutcheons tell,
Long since by one Sir John Mitchell,
And called the Ha' in Vaila

The population is but small,,
And numbers twenty-two in all,
One man and many maids are tall,
And all are strong in Vaila.

Though all the men can use the spade
And help by it to win their bread,
Yet fishing is the favourite trade
When weather suits in Vaila.

But weather does not always suit,
And then they patch or sole a boot,
Or make a rivlin for their foot,
Or mend their lines in Vaila.

But when the weather it does suit
Then bolder men are not afloat
Than those that launch a six-oared boat
And rush to sea from Vaila.

Though winds be strong and billows high
Across the tumbling tide they fly,
Whilst calm and watchful is the eye
Of every man from Vaila.

They luff her up or keep away
And while the raging surges play,
While o'er the gunwale pours the spray
But scares no man from Vaila.

And when they run before the gale
They watch the gusts and dip the sail,
And with a wooden shovel bail
The boats that go from Vaila.

In Spring, when fish approach to spawn
And lines must from the deep be drawn,
The crews arise before the dawn
And hurry off from Vaila.

Through rain and sleet they leave the shore,
And toss at sea ten hours or more;
Their rest is short, their labour sore,
But none complains on Vaila.

Death on a billow-top may stand,
With dust in his uplifted hand,
But cannot daunt the hardy band
That works the boats of Vaila.

Here none a doctor need employ,
For all the best of health enjoy
And Christie Thomson like a boy
Enjoys his food on Vaila.

Although eight years beyond four-score,
And rather stiff to pull an oar
He still can work upon the shore
With flail or spade in Vaila.

In Foula he was born and bred,
And though no books he ever read,
He has more knowledge in his head
Than any man on Vaila.

The knots in wood engage his mind,
And which will raise up gales of wind
If built in vessels he can find
And show the men in Vaila.

He also has the gift or knack,
When luck has left a boat or smack,
By magic arts to bring it back,
Though few believe in Vaila..

No Sabbath bell this island reaches,
No parson ever comes and preaches,
Some shift their shirt and some their breeches
To mark the day in Vaila.

Let others seek the crowded town
Where faces wear a frigid frown,
But I would rather settle down
In some retreat like Vaila.

I've dwelt in places in my time
Where grew the orange and the lime,
But I prefer the bracing clime
And breezy cliffs of Vaila.

What splendid views by sea and land
The wild indented crags command,
The isle of Foula, peaked and grand,
Delights the eye from Vaila.

The lofty far famed Fitful Head,
Of which when boys we all have read
Though pleasures keen now mixed with dread
Is visible from Vaila.

The ruined Brough of Culswick too,
The stronghold of some Pictish crew
Upon a crag appears in view
Across the sound from Vaila.

Here let me live, and when I die
Below the sea-pinks let me lie
Where billows break and sea fowls cry
Upon the crags of Vaila."

In 1900 central heating was installed in Vaila Hall by Taylor and Parsons of Bradford. As a curiosity their quotation for the installation, for £176 is shown below.

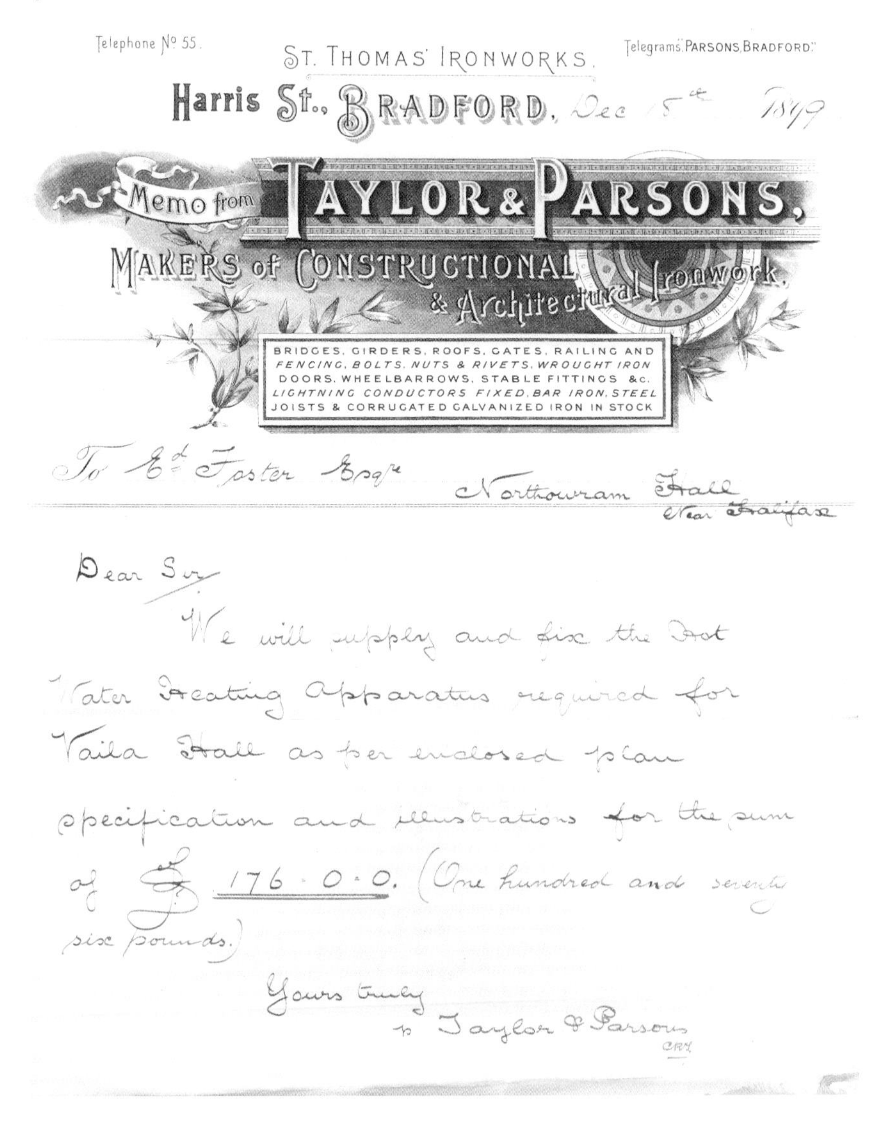

Telephone No. 55. ST. THOMAS' IRONWORKS. Telegrams "PARSONS, BRADFORD."

Harris St., BRADFORD, Dec 15th 1899

Memo from TAYLOR & PARSONS,

MAKERS of CONSTRUCTIONAL & Architectural Ironwork.

BRIDGES, GIRDERS, ROOFS, GATES, RAILING AND FENCING, BOLTS, NUTS & RIVETS, WROUGHT IRON DOORS, WHEELBARROWS, STABLE FITTINGS &c. LIGHTNING CONDUCTORS FIXED, BAR IRON, STEEL JOISTS & CORRUGATED GALVANIZED IRON IN STOCK

To Ed. Foster Esqre Northowram Hall Near Halifax

Dear Sir

We will supply and fix the Hot Water Heating Apparatus required for Vaila Hall as per enclosed plan specification and illustrations for the sum of £ 176.0.0. (One hundred and seventy six pounds.)

Yours truly

p Taylor & Parsons

Christine de Luca is a celebrated poet in Shetland dialect; this poem "Gyaain ta da Eela" (1947) is taken from "A Shetland Anthology" edited by John J. Graham and Lawrence I. Graham 1998.

Gyaain ta da Eela

"Vaila darkenin fae aest ta wast,
        wind faa'n awa;
eela nichts I da simmer dim.

Abon da tide, lik a sell, wir boat wid lie;
we hed ta tize her doon,
bulderin an traan owre da ebb
but nyiff I da sea.

Rowing oot bi wir kent wirld
ta da uncan moo o da Wester Soond,
hols lay black on a sea an sky o gowld.

We'd row til da holm o Burrastow cam close
dan drap da dorro;
een o wis wid aandoo, boos ta da wind.

Waands owre da starn,
piltocks nyddin:
up dey'd come wi a bummel,
sheenin, Spricklin,
dan prammed an pechin at wir fit.

Lines unreffelled
owre da side again
roond and roond da skerry
watching fur froad braking on da baas.
Gleg een, quick hands;
piltocks taakin
bucket fillin
ee mar time
maybe twa.
Dan aathin quiet an da homin closing in.

Packing up wir proil, we'd mak fur hom,
Bbyde o kent lichts. We'd row
peerie wyes, owsin as we god.
Abon wis, tirricks flitin
an a mird of maas laavin an divin,
plotin fur muggies.

We'd rak da boat in on a flowin tide,
dicht an shoard her, dan rin hom prood
i da darkenin wi a fraacht o fish.
We'd aet wir supper
tae tales o uncan Odysseys
in idder voes."

George Mackay Brown is Orkney's most celebrated author and poet. In the company of the much loved Gunnie Moberg he visited Vaila in 1988. He recorded this visit in Northern Lights-A Poet's Sources, edited by Archie Bevan and Brian Murray (1999) as follows.

2 June

"Gunnie drives us to a broken coastline teeming with ewes and lambs,mostly black. How many photographs? A hundred? I should think, more. She goes into a long trance-like dance of picture-taking, on the rocky hill among the lambs that seem to be mostly black.

On the road to Walls, we meet old friends of Gunnie, Sandy and Mary Fraser, farmers, of Culswick. Introductions. "Yes," they tell Gunnie, "Henry's expecting you!" There, soon, at a little jetty, Henry Anderton and his metal boat. We pile in. Again, memory is a liar, it's a cold day, and the sea is cold, and the big Victorian pile on the little steep island of Vaila, built by a Victorian ancestor of Henry, is cold. But Henry piles coal on the stove and pours us generous whisky. (I for one never needed a whisky more for the ghost inside me is quaking in its cage of bones.). The others go with Henry to visit the crags of Vaila, and I crouch over the stove and in the whisky glow think it is a pleasant and easy thing to let another prose-poem flow out. Bacchus and Apollo are not really friends. What I wanted to write was a lilting lyrical piece about the first fiddle in Shetland, that land of fiddlers. Nothing came right: the images tangled with one another and, tugged this way and that, became hard knots.

At last, voices in the hall. The walkers were back, having spanned the small steep island and been suitably impressed with cliffs and horizons and wild birds.

The big house on Vaila is an extraordinary Gothic place, with a great high dining hall hung with ancestral portraits and a minstrels' gallery above. Henry said he might sell it soon. He might go to live in a house nearby, on the main island.

At present, he is a salmon farmer-that new industry has grown very quickly all over the west and north of Scotland. One can't help but wonder how, in time, the quality of farmed salmon will be affected, now that their mysterious seven-year circuit from the hatching home river out among the salt cod of North Atlantic streams, then back inerrably to the same fresh water source that bred them, to spawn and die there, is cut out. The salmon peregrination must be akin, somehow, to the force that drives the blood through the veins and keeps the stars in their courses.

There was nothing insipid about the large salmon Henry Anderton set on a silver salver on his broad kitchen table. We ate it, hunger honed by sea air, with salad and white wine. I forgot about my second ruined poem.

Then Henry boated us back, not the short crossing, but right round Vaila, through a natural rock arch of primitive and awesome savagery such as you find nowhere in tame Orkney. I feel, as the metal boat champs the sea, spume-snorting, and a cold Atlantic wind comes at us, and we go in under the black cliffs of Vaila, the way an average eighteenth century man felt about mountains, crags and torrents: that a town street with folk coming and going, a house and a decent garden of herbs and roses, a fire and book and viol-these were the gifts that society has wrested from the mindless ageless savagery of Nature, a precious perilous heritage. (Wordsworth then was still in his cradle.)

As Henry's boat turned the last cliff buttress, though, a small wild bird was beginning to cry in the spirit.

Foula, the most remote of the Shetlands, was in the north-west distance. (An uncle of mine that I never knew was once the resident missionary there.)

Back at Grobsness, John Somerville arrived with a gift of four trout he'd just caught."

In 1970 Sir John Betjeman paid a clandestine visit to Vaila. In 1971 he wrote to Margaret Stewart's mother, after Henry Anderton had inherited the island in 1971 as follows.

20th April, 1971

Dear Mrs. Dennis,

I went and looked at Burrastow last year and we went over to Vaila Isle. Miss Foster was in bed and we were allowed to tip toe through the house. I am enchanted to know that Vaila is coming to life again. I can think of few nicer places in the world than it and Burrastow. It is worth being alive to have known Shetland.

Yours sincerely,

Mike Finnie wrote the seminal guide to Shetland architecture "Shetland – an illustrated architectural guide" in 1990. The extract on Vaila is as follows.

ISLAND OF VAILA

Burrastow House

from 1973 as the architect's weekend house. The roof has been raised with a strip of glazing inserted around the old wallhead, a glass bay taking the place of the expected central porch. Two derelict horizontal watermills remain at the roadside before **Burrastow House**, 1759, now hotel. Another haa, two storeys on a raised basement, the porch reached by a fore-stair. A seat of the Henrys, the house was bought, altered, and extended, in the early part of this century by Col Foster, a Yorkshire mill-owner, as a summerhouse.

38 **Island of Vaila**

Granted to Robert Cheyne in 1576 by James VI *'to big ane hous and fortice upoun the saidis landis of Valay for sauftie thairof fra the hiland men, perattis, and otheris invasionis...'* Vaila passed from the Cheynes to James Mitchell of Girlsta, a Scalloway merchant. He built the Old Haa in 1696. Passing by descent to the Scotts of Melby, Vaila was sold, in 1893, to Yorkshire mill owner Herbert Anderton. Wool-buying brought him to Shetland. With his brother, he developed Vaila as a farm and the haa was expanded as the family summer residence. House parties were entertained in lavish style; fishing and shooting. (Plans to add a further wing to the house and to build a chapel to seat 100, when the island's population was 30, were abandoned c.1915.)

A contemporary photograph of Vaila Hall, the old Haa forming the right wing

Vaila Hall, 1696 and 1895-1900

Divided from open landscape only by its terrace, with steps guarded by stone griffins. To the old haa as the southern wing, Anderton added the parallel north wing and walled the space between for the baronial hall. All heavily castellated externally, the new wing terminates in a massive round tower, and pepperpots have corbelling in imitation of that at Scalloway and Muness Castles. St Magnus and St Rognvald, portrayed in leaded glass, flank the entrance. The Baronial hall is rich, complete with a minstrel gallery and massive fireplace and

56

SANDNESS

furnished in Jacobean style with all the trappings of the house's heyday preserved *in-situ*. The old moulded entrance to the haa now leads from the hall and retains the armorial panel of the Mitchells above. Commanding the entrance to Vaila Sound, the clifftop **Lookout Tower** is two storey, reconstructed to its present Baronial form by Anderton. It was said to have been used by previous lairds to oversee their own smuggling activities, shipping in goods from French and Dutch vessels. Anderton travelled to the Far East and brought back to Vaila a Buddha and oriental artefacts with which he fitted out a **studio** in a reconstructed boathouse to become what must have been Shetland's one and only Buddhist temple (demolished). **Cloudin Farmhouse**, 1894, is a chunky square house with crowstepped gables. Four clustered chimneys emerge from the centre of the ridge influenced by Arts & Crafts styling. On the beach below the Hall remain the shells of old fishing lodges from Andersons' fishing station.

Left *The Hall, Vaila.* Above *Vaila Tower*

39 **Sandness**: *'a beautiful flat of Corn, Grass, and Meadow ground, facing the west.'* **St Margaret's Kirk**, 1792, is tiny but disused. On the east gable is a weathered stone: *'Fear God 1645'*. Some old grave slabs and 19th century wooden grave markers.

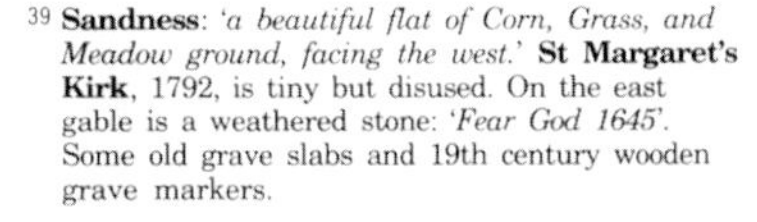

Melby House, c.1800

The usual haa of two storeys with a garret, and additions to the rear. **North House**, 18th century, probably preceeded Melby as the seat of the Scotts, when John, second son of John Scott of Gibliston (Fife) inherited Melby, Vaila and Foula through his mother Grizel Mitchell in 1736. Moulded skewputts are its only relief.

Arthur Anderson of P&O leased Vaila in 1837, and set up a fishing enterprise to provide a market and employment for local fishermen. He hoped to break the hold of the lairds and merchants, who made fishing a condition of tenure by their tenants. Commitments elsewhere made Anderson unable to continue and the enterprise folded, but the fishermen had had a taste of a less restrictive practice.

57

Here are the particulars of Valkyrie, the Vaila teak launch built in 1898, in Phillips auction of Traditional River Craft and Ephemera at Henley in 1995

129

129 VALKYRIE. A Steam Launch

Principle Dimensions: Length: 30ft.; Beam: 6ft. 9in.; Draft: 2ft. 9in.

An open steam launch built by J. Samuel White of Cowes in 1898 of teak planking on American Elm, fastened by copper nails clenched over roves, with stem and stern posts of English Oak, the hull varnished throughout inside and out with cream boot-top and green water-line.

General Arrangement: 7ft. foredeck with bronze fairleads and bollard cleats, airtight forepeak with access hatch below, forward cockpit for boiler firing with steering by four spoke bronze wheel via cable and pulley, inter-connecting to the bronze tiller. Aft of the boiler and engine, is the 10ft. x 6ft. cockpit with side and aft seating furnished with side and aft deep buttoned burgundy cushions, stern deck with tiller, bronze bollard cleats and fairleads, brass ensign staff with forked tail and support rods.

Engine: A now rare Simpson, Strickland & Co. Ltd. of Dartmouth Triple expansion type with Stephenson Link motion reverse size 3in. + 4¼in. + 7in. x stroke 3½in. of 26 i.h.p. at 700 revolutions per minute. Detailing includes drains to cylinders and valve chests, comprehensive lubrication to all main bearing surfaces via three reservoirs, two of which are wick fed and one pressure fed with in-line pressure feed to the high pressure cylinder. There is a combined air and feed pump from the hot well to the boiler.

78

Boiler: Built in July 1987 by Langley Engineering, with welding to British Standard Specification No. 2790, of Yarrow type three drum water tube, tested to 375lbs. per square in., working pressure 250lbs. per square in. The boiler is lagged in green enamel panels bound in brass, exhaust is by a handsome brass annular funnel. Detailing includes sight glass, pressure gauges at engine and at fire doors, high pressure valve chest gauge, vacuum gauge, whistle, blower, safety valve, regulator and a good set of firing irons.

Current Boiler Certificate Dated 23rd May 1995 extant.
A Current Survey Dated 22nd May 1995 extant.

Included in the inventory is the original auxiliary sailing gear, including mast and gaff-rigged loose footed mainsail, steam lance water tube cleaner, seven bronze stanchions for the canvas dodgers, three canvas dodgers, boat hook, ensign, pram canopy frame, fenders and an all over cover.

The launch has had a meticulous restoration programme during the last three years which has included total refurbishment of the boiler, the engine checked throughout and any necessary work done, new parts fitted where needed, and a new set of fire bars were cast, wooden pattern included. The boat has been revarnished and all bright work is in excellent order and the brass work immaculate.

The launch will be afloat at the Sale with a current N.R.A. Thames Licence.

(£28,000-38,000)

VALKYRIE was built for Herbert Anderton, the Laird of Vaila, one of the Shetland Isles. *"Articles of Agreement made this second day of December 1897 - between Herbert Anderton of Vaila, Shetland on the one part and John Samuel White, East Cowes, I.O.W. Shipbuilders on the other part"* are included with this lot. The launch was for Herbert Anderton's personal use between mainland Shetland and his Island. On his arrival each Summer a cannon was fired as he set foot on Vaila.

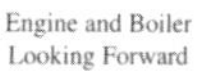

Engine and Boiler
Looking Forward

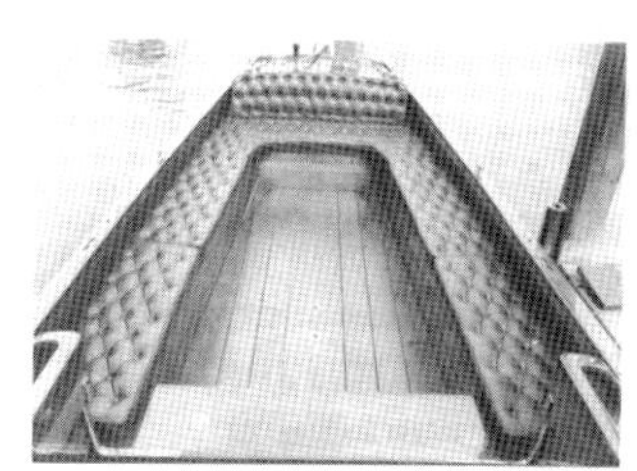

Saloon
Looking Aft

79

As described in Chapter 3 (Early Settlement) we built a 20th century broch for oil storage at our shore-base in Lera Voe. The press release follows. Those from the press making calls for further information were surprised to find themselves speaking to George, our African Grey parrot.

PRESS RELEASE

FOR IMMEDIATE CIRCULATION

First new Broch for 2000 years opens at Lera Voe, Walls

After some 2000 years as archealogical remains, a new use has been found for a broch at Lera Voe. Although a mere 15 ft tall (compared to the 43 ft of Mousa broch), the new broch houses tanks for storing diesel and paraffin, before it is transported for use on the nearby Isle of Vaila. Some modern ideas have been incorporated in the design, such as a roof, an inner insulating breeze block bund and a "baronial" oak door. However it is hard to improve on the exterior design, which gives the new broch its timeless appearance.

The new broch was opened on 24th August by Det. Sup. Val Turner, the pillar of Shetland Archaeology, who said "Archaeology may be the detrius of humanity, but this new broch takes the biscuit".

Alec Wilson, builder, aka Alexander the Great, said "Kiss my highland cock; I built it like the f...er over there" pointing to the Culswick broch.

Freddy Georgeson, Vaila boatman, said "It's a whopper; I won't be able to miss it". His wife, Christine, agreed.

Richard Gibson, architect, said "The formalist functional tradition exhibits itself in a dichotomy when reality encounters fantasy, practicality encounters beauty and the mundane encounters the sublime ...mumble, mumble".

John Abernethy, joiner, said "We built it anyway".

Hamish Thomson, Head of Gardening Dept.,Vaila, said "The fundamental strengths of global permaculture are exhibited in the organic tension of this new broch".

Enquiries

Vaila Press Office 01595 809 363
(ask for George)

Notes for Editors

1. Brochs were constructed by the Picts in the period 200 BC to 200 AD. No firm evidence exists regarding their use; it is unlikely that they were used for oil storage.

2. There is no truth in the rumour that Planning Dept., Lerwick are requiring all oil storage tanks at Sullom Voe to be re-sited in brochs.

As promised this is not a complete "our island story' which must wait for another day. But as a guide for the number of projects available to any aspirant island owner here is a list of our Milestones 1993-2007 and our work-force. Of course we refer to these Milestones as Millstones!

VAILA 1993 - 2007

Milestones

Date	Social	Building	Work Force	Other
1992 October	First visit			
1993	Braer wreck Purchase completed House-warming party	Cottage restored	Freddie & Christene Decorators in summer	Parrot (Voe boat)
1994	Wedding celebrations	Conservatory Electricity Power minder Boiler house (C.H.)	Andrew & Jacqui in cottage & Cloudin Decorators in summer	Pigs arrive (sows) Organic status
1995	First Vaila Open (9 holes)	Central heating Water filtration system	Decorators in summer	Boar arrives
1996	1940s party	Shorebase acquired Potting shed Cloudin Pier	Andrew & Jacqui leave Decorators in summer Hamish in Cloudin	Canary (yellow boat)
1997	Fez & Spectacles party	Broch	Decorators in summer Alec leaves	
1998	Dorota's solo flight to Tingwall, Shetland from North Weald Summer party – Cullivoe dance band	Shorebase finished	Decorators in summer	

Date	Social	Building	Work Force	Other
1999	Tall ships – Polish sailors' visit Vaila Open II (18 holes)	61 Commercial St., Lerwick acquired Vaila Fine Art opens	Hamish & Diane leave Stevie starts as Head of Gardening Decorators in summer at VFA	Vaila organic blankets
2000	Richard's etchings in gallery	Bridge at Ham Road to nowhere West Shed		Whale arrives Highland cattle arrive
2001	Tropical island party	Watchtower harled Bod at 169 Commercial Street acquired	Freddie & Christene leave John takes over as general manager	Bull arrives Monkey (2nd Voe boat) Tamworth pigs
2002	Vaila Open III	Road to Watchtower Environmental Award for Shorebase Watchtower completed Ham pier repairs	Richard S decorates the Bod – moves to Thordale	Ponies arrive
2003		Road to nowhere Environmental Award for Watchtower	Angus on digger Richard S decorates Watchtower	Highland herd reaches 9
2004	Richard's 60th and our 10th wedding anniversary Vaila Open IV Cullivoe Dance Band	Cloudin harled Road to nowhere (cont) Power minder repaired Cloudin harled	Richard S redecorates Cloudin	Coloured Vaila blankets Saddleback boar arrives Love Show at VFA
2005		Road to nowhere (cont) Re-construction of Pier at Ham Cottage redecorated Russian Room decorated	Angus on digger D. Nicolson R. Swales	Allen & Overy Corp Know-how away week-end

Date	Social	Building	Work Force	Other
2006	Turkish delight party at Bod	Road to nowhere (cont) Harling of cottage New generator	Angus Moar Frank Anderson D.H. Marine Ron Sandford – Vaila Series	August – Philip & Eva's wedding in Prague September – Ben & Cassie's wedding in Cornwall Richard wins "Sultana Cake baked by a gentleman" trophy at Walls show
2007	Saree Party at Bod	Harling of West Gable of Hall Road to nowhere (cont)	Frank Anderson Angus Moar Tony Bream – artist in residence	D Day – Johnnie & Arthur born Halloween – Kristina born 8th Birthday party show at VFA

Workforce

Freddie & Christene Georgeson	Boatman and general ops Christene assists with sheep and cleaning 1993 - 2001
Richard Swales Tom Barwood	Decorators from London Summer residents 1993 - 1999
John Abernethy	Joiner from 1995 General Manager from 2001
Stuart Manson	Joiner from 1996 General ops from 2001
Robbie Nicolson	Plumber – C.H.

Jim from Wick	Plumber
Geordie from G&I Nicolson	Plumber & Lead Master: VFA Watchtower
Kenny Watt	Electrician – Vaila Hall
John Isbister	Electrician – VFA, Shorebase, boats
Alec Wilson	Builder 1994-1998
Ian Thomson	Building/General ops from 1996
Andy & Jacqui Hawken	Jewellery, Cannon Stand, VH sink stand, Cottage Dresser General ops 1994 - 1996
Hamish Thomson & Diane Ritch	Gardening/forestry/cooking 1996 - 1999
Stevie Jay	Head of Gardening/Forestry from 1999
Davie Inkster	Dry stone wall at Shorebase
Nicholas Groves-Raines, Edinburgh	Architects – Vaila Hall and island buildings, VFA
Richard Gibson, Lerwick	Architects – Shorebase
Angus Moar	Digger
D. Nicholson	Pier at Ham
Frank Anderson	Harling
Norman Goudie	Plumber
Claire Dalby	Water colourist
Kery Dalby	Lichenologist
D.H. Marine	New Generator
Tony Bream	Artist

As a taster for Volume II, here is an article about our early days on Vaila which appeared in Scottish Field in December 2001.

Survival of the Wittiest

Above: All aboard the Monkey to set sail for Vaila. Inset right: Effie, the Great Dane. Opposite page: Dorota Rychlik and her husband Richard Rowland at home in Vaila Hall.

What does it take to live on an island miles from anywhere? Bridget McGrouther discovers that for the residents of Vaila, eccentricity, wild parties and a very good sense of humour all help...

When Dorota Rychlik, originally from Poland, and her English husband Richard Rowland first moved from London to take up residence on the Island of Vaila off the west coast of mainland Shetland, the locals placed bets as to how long they thought the couple would last living in the remote – and most suspect haunted – old house. Odds were they'd be lucky to stand one winter – perhaps two.

Yet eight years later the resilient pair laugh about the slim chances given for their survival as not only have they settled happily into island life but with the help of local tradesmen – not to mention hundreds of thousands of pounds – they have turned the haunted Vaila Hall into a comfortable home. However, the eccentricities of the couple, complete with their social whirl of weird and wonderful parties including everything from their colourful wedding celebrations to a tropical island extravaganza have kept tongues wagging and many islanders guessing as to what exactly

Photographs Roy Summers

Above: *A painting of Dorota when she was younger.* **Right**: *The cone-roofed ceiling in the boat house is decorated with plywood fish scale tiles.*

goes on on Vaila.

Well, Scottish Field is delighted to announce that we have been privy to the island's inhabitants as well as some of their activities and we can exclusively reveal that Vaila is not an exotic monkey sanctuary, as was strongly rumoured when the couple originally arrived. However, it's easy to imagine why gossip was rife, for Dorota has a wicked sense of humour and encouraged postcards from friends sharing in the joke and requesting such bizarre items as monkey steaks!

Perhaps it takes a certain type of person to be able to leave behind the attractions of a big city and live in the middle of nowhere without at times any water or electricity and no immediate neighbours other than the occasional ghost. Yet when Dorota cheerfully arrives to pick us up in one of her boats – called 'Monkey' for aforementioned reasons – you are soon aware that she is no ordinary person.

Full of life and fun, she bounds ashore with Effie, her pet Great Dane, both displaying subtle signs of a moneyed background – Dorota in Armani specs and the dog sporting a Burberry collar. She's ke 93 show us the transformed boat house, w 'guarded' by a sculptured stone Great Dane.

'We need to have a shore base in case it is

ever too rough, too dark, or we're too tired to make it to Vaila,' Dorota explains.

Inside, the ultra-modern Ikea-type interior has a compact kitchen and upstairs, the cone-roofed bedroom ceiling is decorated with plywood fish scale tiles. Outside the fuel container has been cleverly disguised in the shape of a broch.

All aboard the Monkey and Dorota takes the helm under the watchful eye of local joiner Stuart Manson. As well as learning to navigate the short, but often very rough crossing to Vaila, Dorota also has a pilot's licence which comes in handy when she needs to fly to London on business. Yet again despite the rumours, there is no private runway on Vaila – she uses the local airport at Tingwall on Shetland, though admits she is 'between planes' at the moment, having just sold her Cessna.

Walking into the grand entrance hall of the house on Vaila couldn't be more different from the contemporary shore base. For it's like stepping right back in time, with pseudo-Jacobean furnishings including a huge dining table and chairs, two billiard-settles, a suit of armour guarding the doorway, restored paintings on the walls and even a large Tiger Moth ornamental plane dive bombing from what looked as high as a 40-foot ceiling.

Richard – dressed in a handspun traditional Prince Charles design Fair Isle waistcoat – comes to welcome us and we're ushered into the large kitchen for a cup of freshly-brewed coffee. The general manager John Abernethy and Ian Thomson – responsible for building and general operations – join the welcome committee. Meanwhile Dorota attempts to explain what attracted her and Richard all the way to Vaila.

'I stayed for two years in Ayrshire while I was studying for my phD and felt a real affinity with the place,' Dorota explains. 'So Richard and I were looking for somewhere in Scotland to restore. Vaila was on Historical Scotland's Buildir~ ~t Risk list, so we thought we'd take a l … /e didn't realise quite how far away it … hough – we came up in a day in winter.'

Dorota and Richard bought the island from

Above: Vaila Hall. **Top left:** *Looking down on the grand entrance hall.* **Centre left:** *Feeding the piglets Mary and Helen.* **Below left:** *The Highland cattle calves Sylvie and Fanny.*

Above: *Dorota in her Lerwick gallery.*
Top: *Dorota uses the watch tower as a reading room.*

Dorota and others staying at the house have been woken in the night hearing ornaments smash for no reason as well as unexplained footsteps . . .

Henry Anderton, whose family had owned the estate for more than a century. Henry and his wife Bo are now 'neighbours', running Burrastowe House Hotel across the water and the couple often cater for Vaila's extravagant parties.

Dorota has just turned 40 – much to her disgust – and spends more time at Vaila than Richard, who has not yet retired from his hectic work as a solicitor, but is planning to soon. She is a fine arts dealer and has opened a gallery on Lerwick where she sells paintings, ceramics and organic produce such as Shetland wool blankets. The pair each married before, but both sadly widowed, were introduced by mutual friends who sat them together at a dinner party.

The house had stood empty for 10 years, but the important thing was that it was watertight and they could move in straight away. Yet it has required a lot of restoration to get it shipshape, including rewiring, decoration and putting in central heating and a water filtration system.

As everything ages so quickly on Shetland because of the severe weather, it's a constant battle and the couple very much appreciate the local support they have received. Many even pitched in when they had the unpleasant task of disposing of a dead whale which was beached ashore last year. Yet Dorota looks on it all as one big adventure – even the ghosts which she's convinced haunt the house.

Dorota and others staying at the house have been woken up in the night hearing ornaments smash for no apparent reason as well as unexplained footsteps . . .

Nevertheless, Dorota clearly loves her island home and proudly takes 95 a tour of bedroom after bedroom, bath fter bathroom down long dark corridors decorated with paintings – many of her when she was younger as her previous husband was an artist.

Outside, we get to meet the Highland cattle calves – Sylvie and Fanny – as well as cute red piglets, named Mary and Helen after John the manager's children as they both have red hair! There are also Shetland sheep and Tamworth pigs and Dorota is proud of the island's organic status.

Transport around the mile-square island is by quad and trailer bumping around at sometimes interesting angles near the edge of cliffs to see their private graveyard, the other quay and the watch tower which has also been restored at great cost. There is a bird's eye view of the house and island from the renovated roof and Dorota also points out the 18-hole golf course with challenging near-vertical greens. Hardly surprisingly, numerous golfballs are lost at sea during the Vaila Open Championships.

'Guests either love or hate Vaila,' says Dorota. 'We have single-handedly quadrupled the air traffic at Tingwall, though, mainly due to my flying school friends coming up to see us.

'We don't live at Vaila all year round, so we probably have the best of both worlds, but I find it quite a culture shock when I go back to London now. Mind you, I'm not quite sure what you'll have made of your visit here!'

Well, very definitely eccentric, certainly memorable and really great fun. Vaila may have to be seen to be believed, but believe us, it's worth seeing! □

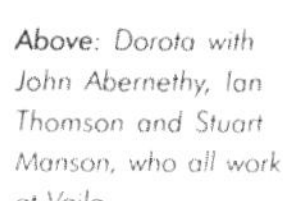

Above: *Dorota with John Abernethy, Ian Thomson and Stuart Manson, who all work at Vaila.*
Below: *Extravagant clothes hang in the bedroom.*
Bottom: *A polar bear skin decorates one of the many guest bedrooms.*

Our thanks to Loganair for our flights from Edinburgh to Shetland.

Footnotes and Acknowledgements

Chapter 1 – The Isle of Vaila

The story of Ragnald Simonsdatter's spat with Thorvald Thoresson is fully described in *Papa Stour and 1299* edited by Barbara E Crawford (2002) and the *Biggins, Papa Stour, Shetland* by Barbara E Crawford and Beverley Ballin Smith (1999). Despite my legal training, and reading the relevant sections several times, I still cannot understand what the dispute was about.

A critique and new translation of the Ballad of Hildina appears in *The Early English Settlement of Orkney and Shetland* by Graeme Davis (2007) to whom I am indebted for his ideas on early English settlement and language in Shetland. Brian Smith's review in *The Shetland Times* of 9th May 2008 and Michael Barnes' review in the *New Shetlander* for Simmer 2008 set about a trenchant demolition of a number of these, but they still appeal to me. Graeme Davis has responded to Michael Barnes in the Hairst edition of the *New Shetlander* 2008. Dorota read English philology at Lodz University, Poland, and linguistics at University College, London, and wrote her PhD thesis on the Relevance of Beauty. She tells me that linguists and philologists can never agree. I guess they sing off different song sheets. I think that without new ideas we will all atrophy.

Chapter 2 – Auld Rocks

The geology of Shetland seems unnecessarily complicated for such a small land-mass; my simplification does not do justice to the subject. Read *Shetland* by Jill Slee Blackadder (2003), overall an excellent introduction to Shetland, and *Shetland – A Naturalist's History* by J Laughton Johnson (1999) for fuller and better descriptions.

Thanks to Jill Slee Blackadder and Allen Fraser for permission to include the geological map of Shetland.

See Hamish Haswell-Smith's seminal *Scottish Islands* to put Vaila in context. From this book, it appears that Vaila is possibly the largest Scottish island solely owner occupied.

Chapter 3 – Early Settlement

In addition to the books referred to under Chapter 2, *Ancient Shetland* by Val Turner (1998) has been my main source.

Thanks to Val Turner and Shetland Amenity Trust for permission to include the maps of pre-historic houses and cairns, burnt mounds and brochs, and to RCAHMS to include the 1853 sketch of Burgi Geos in Yell.

I am indebted to Graeme Davis (in the Early English Settlement of Orkney and Shetland referred to under Chapter 1) for the ideas about Hengist and Horsa, and the advent of the early English, "i-mutation" and so on. This has also been criticised by Val Turner in *Shetland Life* – March 2008, with a response from Graeme Davis in the May 2008 edition.

The story of Ragnhald Simmunsdatter is described in the book referred to under Chapter 1.

Chapter 4 – An Abstract of Title to Vaila

For this Chapter I am indebted to the excellent work and scholarship of John H Ballantyne and Brian Smith in *Shetland Documents 1195-1579* (1999) and *Shetland Documents 1580-1611* (1994) and of Gordon Donaldson for the *Court Book of Shetland 1615-1629* (1991). These provide remarkable insight into life then, and the clear presentation of the texts makes life very easy for the amateur reader. References in the footnotes below to SD1 are to *Shetland Documents 1195-1579* and to SD2 are to *Shetland Documents 1580-1611*, so you can follow the story in the original texts if you want to.

Thanks to John R Baldwin and the Scottish Society for Northern Studies for permission for the quotation from *Shetland's Northern Links – Language and History*.

Thanks to the Estate of Ian B Stoughton Holbourn and Birlinn Limited for permission to quote from the *Isle of Foula* by Ian B Stoughton Holbourn (2001).

The genealogy of the Scotts of Melby comes from Zetland County Families in the Shetland Archive.

Thanks to the Shetland Archive for permission to reproduce the early Conveyance of Vaila.

The early photos of Vaila come from the Shetland Museum Photographic Archive collection. Thanks to them for permission to reproduce them. There are many more in their excellent collection which you can view on line.

Footnotes in the text are to –

1 SD1 Item 32
2 SD1 Item 25
3 SD1 Item 26
4 SD1 Item 27
5 SD1 Item xvii
6 SD1 RSS vii no 502
7 SD2 Item 60
8 SD1 Norsk Rigs-Ragistranter 571/2 581/2
9 SD1 Item 42
10 SD2 Item 71
11 SD2 Item 85
12 SD2 Item 219 ref to SD1 Item 221
13 SD2 Item 243
14 SD2 Item 324
15 Shetland Archive D 10/8/1-4

Chapter 5 – Flora and Fauna

Read *Shetland Lichens* (2005) by Kery Dalby and Claire Dalby for a greater understanding of these amazing organisms, part algae and part funghi.

Chapter 6 – Images of Vaila

Thanks to all the artists mentioned for permission to reproduce their work.

Thanks to John Coutts for providing his aerial photograph of Vaila.

Thanks to Didier Piquer for permission to reproduce his photograph of Vaila from Burrastow.

Thanks to the estate of Gunnie Moberg for permission to reproduce her photograph of Vaila Hall.

Chapter 7 – A Vaila Miscellany

Thanks to Graeme Davis and Birlinn Limited for permission to quote his translation from *Nennius' History of Britain*, his translation of the Ballad of Hildina and extracts relating to the Cunningsburgh Phrase and From the Eagle Song from Early English Settlement in Orkney and Shetland.

Thanks to William Charlton and The Shetland Times for permission to quote extracts from *Travels in Shetland 1832-52* by Edward Charlton.

Thanks to the Estate of I.B. Stoughton Holbourn and Birlinn Limited to reproduce extracts from *The Isle of Foula*.

Thanks to The Shetland Times for permission to reproduce the article regarding emigration from Vaila in *Local news – Vol 1 – The Emigration Years* compiled and edited by Malcolm Hulme.

Thanks to Llanesch Publishers/Folklore Society for permission to reproduce the extract from *County Folklore Vol III* about cats on Vaila.

Thanks to Christine de Luca and Shetland Publishing Company for permission to reproduce Christine de Luca's poem "Gyaain to da Eela" from *A Shetland Anthology*.

Thanks to the estate of George Mackay Browne and John Murray (Publishers) for permission to reproduce extracts from *Northern Lights – A Poet's Sources* by George Mackay Brown

Thanks to Mike Finnie and the Royal Incorporation of Architects in Scotland for permission to reproduce the extract about Vaila from *Shetland – an illustrated architectural guide* by Mike Finnie.

Thanks to Phillips for permission to reproduce the extract from their sale particulars from 1995 relating to Valkyrie.

Thanks to Margaret Stewart for permission to reproduce Sir John Betjeman's letter.

Thanks to the Scottish Field for permission to reproduce the Article on Vaila from *Scottish Field* December 2001.

Back cover

Thanks to Dave Donaldson for permission to reproduce his Navigational Map and for designing the Vaila logo.